WALTER BAGEHOT

Life and legacy

Janet Seaton & Barry Winetrobe
Langport & District History Society

Original illustrations by Mike Sammons

2026

FOREWORD

Tuesday 3 February 2026 marked the bicentenary of the birth of Walter Bagehot in Langport, Somerset. He was one of the towering figures of the Victorian era, the most famous editor of *The Economist,* and the writer of standard classics on British government, the constitution, banking and finance, that remain influential to this day. His articles covered an even wider range of subjects, often from a biographical perspective, including history, poetry, economics and social anthropology.

In the century and a half since his unexpectedly early death at the age of 51 in 1877, there have been about half a dozen or so full biographies – not a great number, it could be argued - including a recent finance-focussed one, and even an imagined autobiography. In addition, there have been numerous articles, essays and other writings about aspects of his work, as well as various collections of his writings (the latter are examined in a later chapter). So why a new study of Bagehot?

This book is intended to be not just another biography, albeit one with access to new material, but also a record of the various means undertaken since his death to commemorate his life and preserve his work and legacy for posterity. The authors believe that this is the first time that such a comprehensive record of this kind has been brought together in one source, and we hope that this focus will be of some utility not just those interested in Bagehot, but to local historians, heritage bodies and others.

One reason for a new study now is that this age of unprecedented access to information regularly supplies new material on the Bagehot story and its interpretation. Another is that recent decades have provided several prominent opportunities for his writings to be cited and exploited, including the great financial crash of the early 2000s, the apparently endless upheavals in British politics, and, even more so, in the British monarchy. Yet, despite these, there remains the apparent paradox between Bagehot's enduring influence and importance and his relative lack of public celebrity.

However, the mainspring for this present volume is the unique perspective of examining Bagehot from his own home town of Langport, and through that lens, not just to examine his life and career as it developed to national and international importance, but to tackle the conundrum that one 1960s writer, Jacques Barzun, described as his being "'well-known' without being known well." Allied to this is the question of his legacy, and how and to what extent he is, or should be, commemorated.

This last question is of especial significance for Langport, where he has been, until relatively recently, practically invisible. The authors, who came to Langport in 2007, assumed that such a small town would mark a citizen who is known, to some degree, worldwide, nearly 150 years after his death. Why was he not? Even at county level, Somerset seemed to do little to mark or even recognise his existence. The authors, along with others in the local community, have sought to rectify this situation, initially through the creation and activities of the Bagehot Memorial Fund, now subsumed into the Langport & District History Society, and now with this book.

A NOTE ON SOURCES AND CITATIONS

As this book is intended to be read by the interested lay reader, as well as for any academic research purpose, notes and citations have been kept to a minimum. At the end of this book we have provided references to the sources used within each chapter, for those who wish to pursue the relevant matter further.

Below you will find a short list of the main sources used and cited throughout the book. As virtually all of Bagehot's works, and many of the key writings about him, are contained in Norman St John-Stevas's *The Collected Works of Walter Bagehot* 15-volume set (1965-86), it is convenient to cite or refer to them as they appear in that collection rather than in their original publications or earlier collections, unless stated otherwise. That Stevas collection also has a number of 'general information' volumes, such as a biography (in vol 1), an extensive set of letters in date order (in vols 12 & 13; some of Walter's grandmother's letters on his early years are in vol 15), and two volumes of 'Miscellany', including notes on Bagehot's appearance, his homes, will and likenesses, as well as an extensive bibliography (in vols 14-15). The full text of the Stevas collection is available online at www.langportheritage.org.uk.

The archives relating to Stuckey's Bank at the NatWest Group Archives, Edinburgh have been extensively used in this book, but, for convenience, detailed references and citations to individual records are not given here.

The original spelling and punctuation in direct quotes from letters and other contemporary records has been retained unless expressly noted otherwise.

As they are liable to change over time, full URL addresses are avoided as far as possible.

Main sources cited

Diaries Surviving handwritten diaries and journals of Eliza Bagehot, 1851-1921, which include lists of letters written and received, often with brief notes on their content. Unpublished.

CWWB Norman St John-Stevas. *The Collected Works of Walter Bagehot*. 15 vols. London: *The Economist*, 1965-86.

Westwater Martha Westwater. *The Wilson sisters: a biographical study of upper middle-class Victorian life*. Athens, Ohio: Ohio University Press, 1984.

EB Life Emilie Barrington. *The Life of Walter Bagehot*. London: Longman, 1914 (reissued as vol 10 of *The Works & Life of Walter Bagehot*, 1915). This biography also includes the text from a few letters not otherwise reproduced in the CWWB volumes.

Grant James Grant. *Bagehot: the life and times of the greatest Victorian*. New York: W W Norton, 2019.

RDE   Ruth Dudley Edwards. *The Pursuit of reason: The Economist 1843-1993*. London: Hamish Hamilton, 1993.

Langport & District History Society website

The History Society's website includes a dedicated section on Walter Bagehot (www.langportheritage.org.uk). Regularly updated, it is intended to develop as both a general introduction to Bagehot for casual readers, and as a dedicated resource for those more interested in his life and work, through the free and full-text access to resources such as the digitised version of the 15-volume Stevas *Collected Works* set, as well as to other archives and artefacts in its 'Bagehotiana' collection.

A note from the artist

The artist has been flattered to be asked to contribute to this volume. He usually paints landscapes and portraits, but the brief proved an irresistible challenge. There is only a single image of Walter Bagehot, a striking portrait now in the National Portrait Gallery, so for this project it has been necessary to invent a great deal. The authors encouraged the artist to use his imagination, whilst occasionally pointing out historic anomalies. On his part the artist has aimed for a degree of historical accuracy, blended with plentiful licence in how the visual information is presented. This has mostly involved inventing colour for the original black and white sources, and occasionally using techniques derived from collage. It was fun to do.

Mike Sammons

The artist's depiction of Walter Bagehot

TABLE OF CONTENTS

Part One: His life

Part Two: His writings

Part Three: His commemoration

KEY CHARACTERS

Bagehot, Edith (c.1786-1870)
Walter's mother. She was born Edith Stuckey, sister of Vincent Stuckey, who led Stuckey's Bank from 1807-1845. She married first, Joseph Prior Estlin, and second, Thomas Watson Bagehot, Walter's father.

Bagehot, Edward (1803-1888)
Walter's uncle, Thomas Watson's brother

Bagehot, Eliza (1832-1921)
Walter's wife. She was baptised Elizabeth Wilson, known as Eliza, eldest of the six daughters of James & Elizabeth Wilson (née Preston).

Bagehot, Thomas Watson (1795-1881)
Walter's father. Director of Stuckey's Bank.

Bagehot, Watson (1824-1827)
Walter's older brother.

Bagehot, Watson (1830-1881)
Walter's cousin. He was the son of Charles Bagehot, one of the Devon Bagehots, a naval officer stationed in Ireland. After his mother's death he was taken in by Walter's parents and brought up as one of the family.

Barrington, Emilie (1841-1933)
Walter's sister-in-law. She was born Emilie Wilson, youngest of the six sisters. She married Russell Barrington.

Hutton, Richard Holt (1826-1897)
Walter met him at University College London and they became close friends and colleagues. Hutton edited many of his collected works after Walter's death.

Wilson, James (1805-1860)
Walter's father-in-law. He founded *The Economist*.

PART ONE

HIS LIFE

CHAPTER ONE

Why is he not better known?

On 14 April 1875, Walter Bagehot wrote to his wife that on the previous day the prestigious and exclusive Athenaeum Club "quite cheerfully" elected him a member, under its Rule 2, which provided a fast-track road to membership for a very limited number each year, who "have attained eminence in Science, Literature, the Arts or for public services." Though obviously pleased with this honour, he mused, "I wonder in which *my* eminence is."

This is perhaps one of several questions about the place of Walter Bagehot as a 'great man', worthy to this day of some degree of both celebration and commemoration. Does he deserve to be better remembered than he apparently has been, especially in the last century or so? Why has he not been more remembered? And what exactly should he be remembered for? It is the second question that is the most interesting.

When he died unexpectedly on 24 March 1877, at the comparatively young age of 51, at the height of his powers, he received a wide and generous outpouring of tributes and appreciation, not just in the press but at all levels, from his home town's Corporation to the two Houses of Parliament. Yet, despite efforts to embed his legacy by his family and friends, especially by having collections of his extensive writings published, his name and his work quickly faded from what wider public appreciation it had attained, even as his influence remained, even grew, in several key areas of life, from government and politics to banking and finance.

By the turn of the 20th century, admirers were writing about this apparent enigma. The writer of one perceptive article in a 1908 journal, began thus:

> It is a curious question why fame should sometimes be so disproportionate to real influence. Many a reader will, I am sure, say on looking at my title, 'Who on earth is Walter?'. And there would be a good deal of sceptical amazement if I replied, 'He was one of the most influential men in England throughout the third quarter of the nineteenth century.' Yet it is true. ... Many men who have never heard of Bagehot are now using his ideas, which smaller men have minted into common coin – sometimes his very words.

This situation was even more apparent in 1926, the centenary of his birth. While this anniversary was marked in a number of journals, and his life and legacy lauded, the enigma was again posed, and explanations attempted.

In later decades, there have been valiant attempts to redress the balance and propel Bagehot towards the front line of greatness. But these have been controversial, as when, in 1937, the eminent historian of the Victorian era, G M Young, pronounced Bagehot, 'the greatest Victorian' (a title conferred also on him by his most recent biographer, the American financial writer, James Grant, in 2019).

One recent admirer, the writer, historian and biographer of *The Economist*, Ruth Dudley Edwards, shrewdly suggested that some of these efforts may even have been counter-productive. She was referring to the publication of the mammoth 15-volume *Collected Works* edited by Norman St John-Stevas for *The Economist* in the second half of the last century, with the launches of various sets of its volumes in the 1970s and 1980s being performed by sitting or former Prime Ministers (just as his Blue Plaque during that period was unveiled by the then Premier, Harold Wilson). She wrote, in the introduction to her 1993 collection of his greatest and most quotable writings, *The best of Bagehot* (her own effort 'to spread the light'), "Perhaps such attention from the great and good merely serves to give an impression of Bagehot as the object of veneration of 'an army of fogies'."

Despite all this, and even being mentioned in a successful Netflix series, *The Crown*, Walter Bagehot remains hardly a household name, even though his underlying influence endures. He has a degree of worldwide fame, with many things, even an asteroid, named after him. He has – albeit belatedly, in 1967 - his Blue Plaque. When the Royal Mint issued souvenir coins to celebrate the 2012 London Olympics, a quote from Bagehot featured alongside those from such luminaries as Shakespeare and William Blake. But, not surprisingly, he didn't even make the top 100 of 'Great Britons' in the much-publicised 2002 BBC poll. In 1998 Roger Kimball, a notable editor and publisher, wrote that "Bagehot is one of those distinguished literary figures who seems to have been embalmed by his own distinction."

Possible reasons

Many reasons have been suggested over the last century and a half why this should have been the case. Here are some of the most obvious and likely ones.

Perhaps the primary reason is his unusual surname. How do you pronounce Bagehot? Because no audio evidence exists, reliance must be placed elsewhere, and many suggestions have been made. For the record, we accord with the views of recent serious Bagehot scholars, such as Norman St John-Stevas and Ruth Dudley Edwards, that it is pronounced with a soft 'g', as in 'badge', hence 'badge-it' or perhaps 'badge-ot'. The correct phonetic spelling of 'Bagehot' is bædʒət (or, in a more modern variant, badʒət). It is easy when confronted with an unusual name to avoid it as much as possible, rather than risk public ridicule for mispronunciation. This sometimes seems to be true in and around Langport itself, which may account in part for the relative absence of commemoration there.

His future Wilson in-laws had problems when first encountering Walter in 1857 at the country home: "We agreed 'that Mr. Bag-*hot* must be arriving'. We did not know how to pronounce his name." Later that year, Walter wrote to his then fiancée, Eliza Wilson, "I have in my head at this moment exactly how you desired me to write down my name that you might be able to spell it."

Stevas said in a 1969 BBC broadcast that when he met Pope Paul VI, the pontiff not only admitted not knowing of Walter Bagehot, but also mispronounced his name. He went on to admit that "His Holiness, alas, is not alone in ... the mispronunciation of his name, which is almost universal, and against which I fight a continuing but probably losing battle."

Pope Paul VI

That Bagehot died both prematurely and unexpectedly, gave him not the instant celebrity of the tragic hero, but the risk of relative obscurity. Though his output was prodigious, especially in magazine articles and journal essays, most of it was produced over a relatively short period of just over 20 years, from the mid-1850s to the mid-1870s. This is all the more remarkable in view of his life-long struggle with poor health. In his final years, he had been focussed on more substantial works, but they were never completed. It would have been relatively simple to dismiss his output as ephemeral, important for his immediate time, but not weighty enough for enduring fame.

Also, for all his contemporary fame, he lived and operated within a very narrow, albeit important, circle of metropolitan society. *The Economist*, the magazine he edited for many years with such élan, and similar publications, were influential among their elite readerships, but these rarely numbered more than the few thousands. It was all too easy for a key figure in such a small pond to disappear over time.

Perhaps most damning in this context is the sheer range of Bagehot's work. Operating largely as a journalist and editor, his job was to produce instant copy on matters of current public interest. If alive today, he would probably be a highly respected 'pundit' on the various print and electronic media available – but do such personalities endure? We like nowadays to be able to describe and define a person in a very few words, but with Bagehot that is impossible. Even in his politics, though he stood as a Liberal candidate for Parliament, he was both described as a 'conservative Liberal' and a 'liberal Conservative'.

He was a practical person, who saw events and issues from a practical perspective, most obviously in the field of finance, where he had years of on-the-ground experience as a practical banker. He was certainly not, and would probably have been pleased not to be, an academic theorist, writing weighty tomes. He did write several important books, but they either largely grew out of his essays – as with *The English Constitution* - or his own expertise – as with *Lombard Street*. He was thus open to charges of shallowness, a writer of works not based on original research and evidence.

One might expect someone who wrote engagingly about a wide range of subjects from literary criticism to history (usually through the medium of biographical profiles), and even what may now be termed social anthropology, as well as his core areas of politics and finance, to be lauded as a polymath or renaissance man. Sadly, too often such people are dismissed as 'jacks of all trades' and masters of none, lacking the necessary depth to be enduring. Allied to this indictment is the charge that he is *too* quotable – a criticism apparently not applied to the greater gods like Shakespeare, Wilde or Johnson.

Finally, for modern audiences, he can appear as what Ruth Dudley Edwards pithily described as a "solemn Victorian worthy", assumed therefore to be dull, wordy and boring; writing about, as she put it, "an odd range of heavy-sounding subjects under deadly titles." This perception is compounded by the only existing image of him looking serious, complete with full beard and moustache. It is an image that can be hard to get beyond.

So, Walter Bagehot is a puzzle. When we started writing and giving talks about him more than a decade ago, we described him as 'Langport's unknown celebrity'. He had a degree of fame and recognition, but, in our view, and that of his many admirers, not to the extent he merited. He is someone certainly worthy of greater commemoration – within Langport, and Somerset, to start with - even if perhaps not of unalloyed celebration, given that some of his views, though standard for his time, would be regarded as outdated or even abhorrent today.

As to the other two questions posed here – does he deserve to be better remembered, and, if so, for what? – this work aims to address them, but it is up to its readers how they would answer them.

His father, Thomas Watson Bagehot – perhaps a genuine candidate for 'solemn Victorian worthy' as a banker and civic leader in little Langport – had, near the end of his life, and in failing health, not followed Walter's successful career as closely as he had in previous times. On seeing and hearing the tributes that poured in following his death in 1877, he remarked, with some surprise, "I should never have known how great a man Walter was had I not survived him."

CHAPTER TWO

Bagehot's background

Some sources claim that the Bagehots came to England with William the Conqueror, since the name Bagott is on the Battle Abbey Roll, a contemporary list of William's companions. Ancestors of more recent times are said to come from Prestbury in Gloucestershire, and to be related to the aristocratic family of Baghott De La Bere. It's a connection that was well known in the family. Walter's wife Eliza records in her diary on 25 May 1876 that Edward Bagehot brought her some "family papers about the Bagehots & De La Bere families of Prestbury, near Cheltenham."

The arms of Baghot of Prestbury

The arms of Baghot and Wilson

The arms of Bagot, or Baghot, of Prestbury ('ermine, on a bend gules three eagles displayed or') are depicted on a painted and framed coat of arms said to belong to Walter Bagehot. They are shown 'impaled by' the arms of Wilson. When Michael Churchman, historian of the Bagehot and Stuckey families, was researching the Bagehot family tree in the 1970s, he checked with the College of Arms, who replied that "there is no record of any grant of arms being made to anyone of the name of Bagehot." The family also adopted a crest. Described as 'a stag's head cabossed sable, between the horns a greyhound courant collared gules,' it can be seen, along with the coat of arms, on the Bagehot headstones in All Saints' churchyard in Langport. On the headstone to Walter's parents, the coat of arms depicts the families of Baghot and Stuckey.

BAGEHOT

The Bagehot crest

However, records to support the connection with the Baghott De La Beres are sparse. There can be a risk that families who wish to be descended from a noble line make unwarranted assumptions, and the regrettable habit of giving children the same first names as their parents makes the definitive identification of individuals doubly difficult. In addition, variations in the spelling of the Bagehot surname add further confusion. There may also have been relevant papers which are now lost.

What can be substantiated is that there were Bagehots living in Abergavenny in the first half of the 18th century. They were stalwarts of the non-conformist Castle Street Chapel for many years. Thomas Bagehott and his wife Anne had five children – two sons and three daughters. While their son William stayed in Abergavenny, their eldest child, Thomas, who was born in 1719, came to Somerset and became known as Bagehot.

The reason for his move is not known, although when he married Priscilla Osler in Thurloxton in 1744, the parish register described him as being from Wiveliscombe. By 1747, however, they had settled in Langport. He was Walter Bagehot's great-grandfather. In the Somerset branches of the family the spelling of the Bagehot surname gradually settled into its modern form.

Described as a maltster, Thomas quickly established himself in business in Langport, living initially in Hill House, opposite the parish church of All Saints, later the residence of the Stuckey family. He went into partnership with George Stuckey, a merchant, and together they built up a thriving river trade between Langport and Bridgwater, employing barges to bring goods such as coal and timber upriver and unloading them at their wharves for onward distribution. This was the first stage of binding the two families together in business – an association which lasted for over 100 years.

Thomas and Priscilla had six children, three boys and three girls. One son, Robert, stayed in Langport and joined the family firm, known as Stuckey & Bagehot. The Company operated out of warehouses at Langport's Great Bow Bridge, and dominated the river trade for nearly a century. The other two sons, Thomas and William, went to Great Torrington in Devon and set themselves up as leather dressers and glovers. Both the Devon Bagehots and the Somerset Bagehots flourished.

Based in Langport, Robert Bagehot, Walter's grandfather, married Mary Watson, the daughter of a Unitarian Minister in Bridgwater. Memorials to the Watsons can be seen in Christchurch Chapel in Dampiet Street, Bridgwater. Robert's father Thomas had also trained as a Unitarian Minister, and this streak of non-conformism shaped much of Walter's life. Robert named his first surviving son Thomas Watson, who became Walter's father. Thomas Watson was one of seven children, so Walter was amply provided with aunts, uncles and cousins. In 1823, when Thomas Watson Bagehot married Edith Estlin, George Stuckey's granddaughter and sister of Vincent Stuckey, the head of Stuckey's Bank, he further reinforced the links between their two families.

Walter was not, however, an only child. His mother, Edith Stuckey, had been married before to Joseph Prior Estlin, the son of a Unitarian Minister in Bristol, who died in 1811. They had had three children, Vincent, George and Joseph, who were therefore Walter's half-brothers. George & Joseph died young, but Vincent, who was mentally handicapped, lived in the family home at Herd's Hill, just outside Langport, until his death in 1869. Walter's parents, Edith and Thomas Watson, had a son called Watson two years before Walter was born, but sadly, he died aged three.

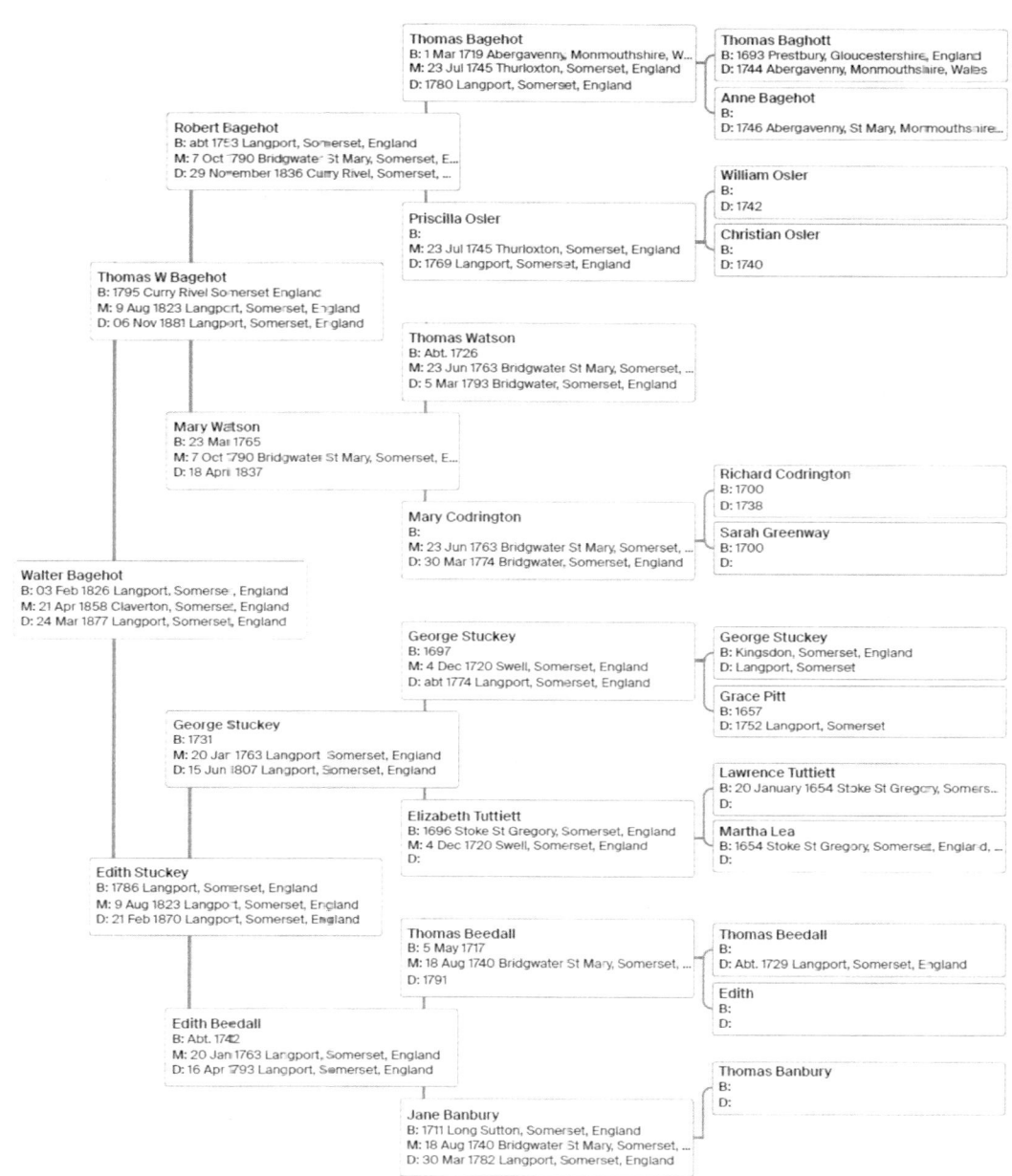

Walter Bagehot's family tree

Walter's parents, Thomas Watson Bagehot and Edith Bagehot (née Stuckey)

Walter became a precious and much-loved child on whom the hopes of his parents were focussed. However, in the winter of 1830-31 his parents took in another Watson, the baby son of his uncle Charles Bagehot, whose wife had just died. Charles was a naval officer who came from the Devon Bagehots, and was stationed in Ireland, near Cork. His son Watson was to become a major force in the family trading business.

Family ties

Walter Bagehot's relatives are not so much a family tree as a thicket. It's impossible to say whether marriages that fostered business links were encouraged, or that business connections brought people together who then formed friendships and perhaps marriages. However it came about, the Stuckeys and Bagehots intermarried to a bewildering extent. Both families had numerous relatives who kept in touch throughout their lives, and this extended family network provided Walter with friendships, support, and a wide social circle that would prove both useful and reassuring in equal measure.

Walter's parents were the great-grandchildren of the Thomas Bagehot and George Stuckey who originally founded the Stuckey & Bagehot partnership. The closeness of the two families, both in business and personal relationships, is remarkable.

Edith Stuckey's uncle Samuel established Stuckey's Bank, and her brother Vincent married Samuel's daughter Julia, his first cousin. Vincent Stuckey developed the Bank into one of the biggest and most trusted banks in the West Country. His reputation also gave Stuckey's Bank a national profile at a time when a robust banking system was becoming key to a successful economy. Thomas Watson Bagehot became a Director and a manager of the Langport branch of the bank, its original headquarters. It was in this building, Bank House, that Walter was born on 3 February 1826. Thus united both in business and by family ties, the Stuckeys and the Bagehots dominated the commercial and social life of Langport in the 18th and 19th centuries.

The Estlin family were also closely related to the Bagehots. Alfred Estlin, a solicitor in Somerton often used by the Bagehots, was related to Walter by marriage on both his mother's and his father's side. Alfred's half-brother, Joseph Prior Estlin, was Walter's mother's first husband, which makes him Walter's step-uncle. Furthermore, Alfred's brother, John Bishop Estlin, married Walter's aunt, Margaret Bagehot.

Joseph Prior Estlin, Edith Stuckey's first husband

Alfred's sister, Anna Maria Estlin, married Dr James Cowles Prichard, a doctor and psychiatrist who was a considerable influence on Walter while he was at college in Bristol. Their son Constantine, therefore a cousin, became Walter's lifelong friend.

Once Walter moved to London he began to get to know some of his more distant relatives. Walter's great-grandmother Priscilla Osler was the sister of Timothy Smith Osler's great-grandfather, so he and Walter were distant cousins. Timothy Smith Osler was a barrister in London, and he and Walter became close friends. Osler was also related by marriage to Walter's great friend, Richard Holt Hutton, who founded the *National Review* with Walter.

Richard Holt Hutton

Walter's aunt on his father's side, Mary Anne Bagehot, married John Stuckey Reynolds, the son of John Reynolds and Ann Stuckey. Ann Stuckey was his aunt on his mother's side, Edith and Vincent Stuckey's sister. John Stuckey Reynolds was a senior clerk in the Treasury. Walter was very fond of his 'Aunt Reynolds', and he saw them frequently when he was in London. They also all went on holidays together.

Walter's marriage to Eliza Wilson, the eldest of six sisters, provided him with another ready-made family circle. He became particularly close to Emilie's husband, Russell Barrington, and Julia's husband, William R Greg, who was a fellow journalist for *The Economist*, as well as Eliza's uncle, George Wilson of Hawick.

CHAPTER THREE

Young Walter

Walter Bagehot was born around 11am on Friday 3 February 1826, in the family home at Bank House, Cheapside, Langport, a building which doubled as the main office of the family bank, Stuckey's Bank, in which his father, Thomas Watson Bagehot, was a senior officer. He was the second child of Thomas and his wife, Edith, the first, Watson, having arrived in 1824. As his latest biographer James Grant, quipped in a 1977 article, "A few people die in banks; no one is born in them."

His grandmother, Mary Watson Bagehot gave her daughter, Mary Anne Reynolds, the details in a letter the day after Walter's birth:

> I have the pleasure to inform you that yesterday morning about eleven o'clock Edith presented us with another very fine boy, not so pretty as Watson it is said but a large handsome fellow who can already make the nursery ring with his strong voice, tho he is generally quiet and with his mother I am happy is going on as well as we can wish ... the little fellow is to be called Walter, a name I like very much, and I already love him dearly, but I shall not suffer him to lessen my affection for my dear boy, who looks at him with great curiosity and likes him very well when Mrs Babbet [the nurse] does not take him - but he will soon get over that objection, as he is a rational little creature.

His early childhood can be glimpsed in fragments from recollections and letters of family and friends. His father was a Unitarian, but despite having a Unitarian birth certificate, Walter was brought up as an Anglican, reflecting his mother's strong faith. For a time in the following summer it was thought that Edith was again pregnant, but it was not to be. At some point while he was still only days or weeks old, he was taken up to Herd's Hill, just to the west of Langport, to witness the laying of the foundation stone of the new house his grandparents were building there, on which work began in February 1826.

Walter, and his older brother, Watson, spent much time with their grandparents, especially in the following summer, as his grandmother described in another letter, of 9 July 1827, to her daughter: "Walter will sit on your father's knee, and I have scarcely a difference in my feelings of affection between him and Watson." However, this family idyll was not to last, as Watson died on 22 October that year. According to a further letter on 14 November: "little Walter is a blessing and a comfort to us all, and when our dear good darling is in some degree faded from our remembrance we shall probably delight ourselves more in him than it is in our power now to do, but never as we did in Watson, *nor ought we*."

Walter indeed became a comfort to his grandparents, especially his grandfather (by then partly blind) as a letter of 21 May 1829 shows: "Walter who is staying with us is a great amusement to him, and is now 8 o'clock Friday morning gone into the garden with him riding on a stick which he calls Jockey Poney." This love of horses became reality, shortly thereafter, as he was riding a pony, Medora, under supervision, by the time he was four.

Walter's half-brother Vincent was not able to join in his physical and intellectual activities, and Watson, adopted at birth by his parents in 1830 from Bagehot cousins in Ireland, was four years younger, so Walter spent much of his time in solitary pursuits.

Walter was able to write at an early age, as an undated family letter from the winter of 1830-31 refers to Walter hoping that a letter of his has been received. His first surviving letter probably dates from 1831, addressed to a great-uncle in Bridgwater, Jacob Watson. Though brief it is full of what must have been important information for a five-year-old: "Is the mast of the *Eritannia* up? [a reference to a new addition to the family's shipping fleet, launched at Bridgwater on 24 September 1831]. The other day I saw a dancing dog. Papa bought me a french polish Gun in Bristol. Baby [a reference to his adopted cousin] begins to talk and papa thinks he will walk by the spring." By June 1832, his grandmother was complaining that Walter was writing his own label on her roses.

Surviving letters from this period demonstrate that, very quickly, Walter was writing detailed and literate letters to his family, and corresponding with his father when one or other was away from home. This practice only increased when Walter went to school, and the parental correspondence took on a new layer of educational content. He was a relatively solitary boy, very attached to his parents and they to him, and this was made more complex and intense as his mother's mental health deteriorated, a problem that plagued the family for decades. There were also early signs of Walter's own health problems, with his grandmother worrying that a persistent cough that was troubling the boy in late 1834, and causing anxiety to his parents, might be a sign that he was inheriting a Stuckey family trait.

Walter could be a precocious child. He used to terrify his mother by climbing to the top of Burton Pynsent Monument, near their home, and running round the coping which was unprotected by any rail or guard. A letter written after Walter's death to his first biographer, Emilie Barrington (a sister-in-law) from Henry Sawtell, a distant cousin of the Stuckeys, contained many reminiscences of Walter from when he first met the family. Notable was an incident from 1835, when Walter was 9: "Mrs. Bagehot rather liked to exhibit her clever boy, who eluded her efforts by swarming up a great tree, and there glaring down on the assembly from the topmost bough in a surprising manner and to the detriment of his Sabbath raiment."

Mrs Barrington said that Walter "lived much in his imagination", and a good example of this was his perception of himself as a swordsman. A June 1833 letter by his father to his 7-year-old son while the family was on holiday at Blue Anchor, near Minehead, on the north Somerset coast, informed him that "your sword is sent, and as to-morrow is the anniversary of the battle of Waterloo, I suppose you will be very grand on the occasion. How would you have liked living at Brussels when the cannons began to roar and the soldiers were summoned to the field?" He would use his sword at Herd's Hill to lash off the heads of flowers with terrible force, imagining himself a great military leader and the demolisher of thousands of Saracens. In the same 1833 letter, his father noted that "Mamma tells me you are becoming a poet and I shall look forward some day or other to our having a 'Sir Walter' in our own family."

Walter began his education at home under a governess, but after that he would have to brave the outside world as he entered formal schooling, at first in Langport, but later in the large cities of Bristol and London.

Young Walter at the top of the Burton Pynsent monument

CHAPTER FOUR

Education

Education was a crucial part of Walter's development. His mother, through her family connections with the Estlins and Prichards of Bristol, was steeped in an intellectual environment, and his father was determined his son would get the education he regretted he did not have, as he explained in a letter to Walter in December 1842:

> The education required in the present day must be laid on a wide foundation, and ample time given for raising the structure. A tree and its roots and branches is a better figure. The roots must be deep and firm if the trunk is to grow high and its branches spread widely, and all its parts must grow together. ... Every day do I feel how much I have lost in not having had such an education as I wish to give you, and you need not therefore fear that anything will be wanting on my part to secure to you its advantages.

Governess

In 1831, when Walter was five, he began his education under Miss Jones, who was engaged as a governess. She remained with the Bagehot family for 40 years, as what Emilie Barrington in her biography describes as "a faithful and confidential retainer", and she appears several times in Eliza's diaries. She introduced young Walter to the works of Dickens and Scott, which may well have laid the foundation for his lifelong love of literature, both as a personal recreation and a subject for his professional writings.

Langport Grammar School

Four years later, when aged around 8 or 9, he was enrolled as a day pupil at Langport Grammar School, an ancient and well-respected establishment in the town. Its able headmaster, William Quekett, ran the school for over 50 years, from 1790 until his death in 1842. In Bagehot's day, the school operated from his home on the south side of Bow Street, in probably what is now Ensor House.

In an advertisement in a local paper in June 1835, Quekett described the school curriculum as comprising instruction in Greek, Latin and French languages; English grammar and composition; geography, history, mensuration, geometry, trigonometry, natural philosophy, algebra, astronomy, and the use of the globes, 'with other branches of useful and general education.' The treatment of pupils was 'liberal' and 'every attention is paid to their religious acquirements and literary proficiency.' To top it all also offered was 'dancing and drawing by approved teachers.'

We know relatively little of his time at the school. In a family letter shortly after he started school, possibly in 1834 (it was dated 22 October but no year was included), he was described as being "much pleased" with his school, was "very industrious" but "as full of fun as ever." His letters to his parents display highly detailed knowledge of a wide range of matters – including the lives of Alfred the Great, St Augustine of Hippo and

Julius Caesar, and the Battle of Marathon - though it is not always clear whether these intellectual exercises derive from studies at his school or at his father's feet.

There seemed to be times when he was struggling with the intensity of his schoolwork, added to what his parents also gave him to learn. He confessed to his mother in a letter in May 1838: "I had not time to do my lessons for you, either today or yesterday, I have been so busy but I think it would rather puzzle me to say what I was about all day yesterday but today I had a very difficult proposition of Euclid, which with the writing out and all kept me nearly two hours."

Ensor House, Bow Street, Langport
Thought to be the original home of Langport Grammar School

In November of that year he wrote to his mother, then in London, about flooding in Langport, a common occurrence then: "The water has got up into the Moor which occasions great commotions in the school for fear it will be too wet to have a bonfire and let off fireworks. T. Paul surmises that they have let the water in because the boys shall not have a bonfire; but the fact wants confirmation, he having, as I can learn, no authority for it but his own thoughts."

The school magazine, *The Alfredian*, writing in 1907 about Bagehot's widow presenting it with a portrait of her husband – a version of the only available image – also reproduced a poem it attributed to him from 1840 about the 'shackling' of eggs on Shrove Tuesday (apparently a school custom at that time). It stated that Walter was at the school in 1840.

The problem with this is that by 1840 Walter was at Bristol College, having moved on from the school the previous year. It is possible that it was written by Walter either in 1840 as an 'old boy' (accepting that the writer in 1907 was in error about him still being there in 1840) or earlier, while still at the school. The more likely answer may lie in the poem's attribution as printed in 1907, "W. Bagehot, 1840", which may refer not to Walter, but to Watson (c1830-1881), Walter's adopted cousin, who was also a pupil at the school.

Bristol College

On Friday 9 August 1839, Walter, aged 13, was taken by his father to his new school, Bristol College. They had travelled via Cheddar, where they had stayed over and had what his father described, in a letter to him shortly after, as "so happy a breakfast." His father had headed back the same way, taking tea at the very same establishment. During that journey back to Herd's Hill, his thoughts were "wholly fixed on you, and with a parent's prayer for your happiness" and he confessed that he had thought of little else since his return.

Bristol College, sited in Park Row, was then a relatively new institution, opened in 1831. It was non-denominational, which would have appealed to his Unitarian father, though his Anglican mother would have preferred him to go to a public school. When writing to his mother in May 1838, Walter confessed to concern at being away from home for up to six months at a time when he went to what he described as "the *heretical* college, as you call it."

The College was described in a city guide of 1840 as being designed to afford boys from the Bristol area and beyond 'the advantages of a classical and scientific education of the highest kind, and on the most moderate of terms. ... The college course includes the classical education afforded at the public schools of Winchester, Eton, Westminster and Harrow; with so much instruction in the mathematics and in ancient and modern literature, as the time to be spent by each student at the college will allow of his acquiring.'

Walter's first letter to his mother from the school, on 19 August, suggested that he was rather thrown in at the deep end. No sooner was Mr Bagehot out of sight than the bell rang, "and I posted off with all convenient speed to do my Virgil, which was not very very hard work particularly as I had done it all before. ... After my Virgil I did my Ellis and the next morning my Kenrick", these being textbooks on Latin and Greek, respectively. His first Sunday was taken up with church, and much preaching.

He boarded with Revd John Bromby, in Park Row, Clifton, the acting principal of the College. He spent much time with local relatives on his mother's side, the Estlins, and especially with the Prichards, who also lived in Park Row at the Red Lodge. Dr James Cowles Prichard was on the Board of the College and also taught a course on the history of civilisation there. At the Prichards, he met many notable scientists and doctors, which probably began his interest in matters scientific, especially in areas of ethnology and social anthropology, as evidenced much later in his career, most visibly in his 1872 book *Physics and Politics*.

He was a dedicated and inquisitive scholar, able to tackle the wide range of sometimes esoteric subjects from French, Hebrew and German to classics (a compulsory subject) and mathematics. His letters home reveal his competitiveness – whether in his own mind, or because of perceived parental pressure - over his rankings in examinations, revelling in his frequent success and regarding relative failures as spurs to greater effort. There exist two 'certificates of honor', dated December 1840, awarded to him for what is termed 'distinguished answering' in classics and mathematics. When the College was forced to close in 1841-2, Walter continued his studies at the little school opened by Mr Booth (the then principal) at his own home at St Michael's Hill.

As if the formal curriculum were not enough for the young teenager, he would take extra private tutoring in maths; read widely – including Shelley ("my restorative"), and Boswell's Life of Samuel Johnson – and attend public lectures on weighty subjects like Zoology, Natural Philosophy and Chemistry.

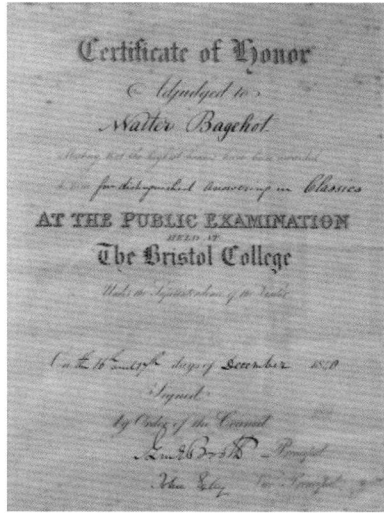 

Bristol College Certificates of Honor for 'distinguished answering in Mathematics and Classics'

His dislike of popular forms of recreation such as sports and games, distanced him from many of his fellow pupils, and from the more social side of education. He also had a distaste for music which lasted almost to the end of his life. He seemed to be developing as a loner and a swot, with an sense of superiority over his schoolmates. One example will suffice. In a letter to his father on 7 December 1839 he revealed that he had declined to go with the other boys to 'Ryan's Circus', which he dismissed as "a kind of low theatre where I believe they act by dumb show; it is also the resort of jugglers, mountebanks, etc etc. A most unintellectual place." More revealing is his admission that if he had been persuaded to go, not only would he have lost several hours of studying time, he would have "acquired the sincere hatred of all the boys for my mugging if I had stayed and passed thereby a faint censure on their amuzement."

He did make a few lifelong friends, such as Edward Fry (1827-1918), of the famous Bristol Quaker chocolate family, and William Killigrew Wait, a future Mayor of Bristol and Tory MP for Gloucester. He was a contemporary of Timothy Smith Osler, a distant relative, whom he later befriended at University College London. Fry later described the Bristol College Bagehot as "lanky youth, rather thin and long in the legs with a countenance of remarkable vivacity and characterised by the large eyes which were always noticeable, and about which he used at one time to entertain amusing conceits."

While at Bristol, he still took an interest in matters back home, such as the family businesses. Writing to his father from Clifton on 24 September 1839, he asked about a boatman's strike, expressing quite strong opinions about this dispute:

> Mamma mentioned in her two last letters a strike for wages among the boatmen; how did it arise; from your having wished to lower, or their having wished to heighten their wages. I should fancy it was rather a serious thing, since those boatmen are not very greatly gifted with the spirit of meekness, and they will be rather apt to vent their rage on those who are

willing to work for the reduced wages. I hope in your promised letter you will give me a full account of the 'rebellion' and its causes and effects.

His letters home also reveal an interest in contemporary politics and government, such as the major political debates over the Corn Laws – with its implications for Free Trade - and the legal battles over parliamentary privilege in *Stockdale v Hansard*. His mother also provided him with tales of metropolitan society during her visits to her brother, Vincent Stuckey's London home. She reported, for example, in a letter of 20 May 1841, attending a concert and sitting behind no less a person as the Duke of Wellington, who "alas! looks quite, quite old and tottery - and decrepit."

Towards the end of his Bristol period, he began to spread his wings a little, including a brief visit in May 1842 (initially against his mother's wishes) to family then in Clevedon, little knowing how important this seaside town would become to him in the future.

Walter's three teenage years in Bristol, away from the security of home, left a lasting impression on him, not just in his intellectual development, but in his maturing character and demeanour, and prepared him for his next stage of education, at university in London.

University College London

In the autumn of 1842 Walter began his formal higher education at University College London. This was probably an inevitable choice, as Oxbridge was in practice unavailable, at least in his father's mind, because of their religious admission tests. UCL also had a more modern approach to teaching – by the lecture rather than the tutorial – and its range of subjects neatly followed on from Walter's Bristol studies.

Nevertheless, London was as dramatic a step up from Bristol in Walter's independent living, as Bristol was from Langport. He lodged with a Dr Hoppus, a classics teacher, at 39 Camden Street. Although Camden Town was then relatively near the more rural parts of the metropolis (like nearby UCL itself), and not far from his Reynolds relatives in Hampstead, it must have been quite a culture shock to the Somerset teenager. Within days of his arrival, he confessed to his mother "to having felt rather dismal when Papa left me at the University in the midst of a thick London fog; and I cannot say but I felt rather dismal occasionally since, when I think of Herd's Hill and you all sitting quietly and happily down amid all its beauties while I am toiling here in the midst of dust and smoke."

His student years in London seemed to be an endless cycle of deep pessimism about his chances of academic success, pre-exam illness, followed by great results in his exams. Whether his illnesses were genuine illnesses, common pre-exam nerves, or, more likely, a mixture of the two, is impossible to know. His state of mind was nearly summed up in a letter to his father in October 1846: "I have never been without fears and I am now entirely without hopes, though as the time draws near my fears increase faster than my hopes."

Ill-health was a constant problem for Walter throughout his life. Even in his early days his family feared that he might have inherited supposed family conditions. These bouts of illness had a major impact on his life, both throughout his education and in his later professional and social life. Ultimately he succumbed to illness at the early age of 51, when he could have had many more years of productive acitivity to look forward to.

There were doubtless periods of genuine ill-health, and he missed long periocs of study during what turned to be a protracted period at university. Notably he skipped the 1843 autumn term – spending much of the months off at home convalescing by riding and hunting - and even postponing taking his BA for a full year in 1845. Not surprisingly, his parents and friends were constantly concerned about his welfare. An extended continental vacation was arranged for him with his aunt and uncle Reynolds in the summer of 1844, when they toured Belgium, Germany and Switzerland, his first ever trip abroad.

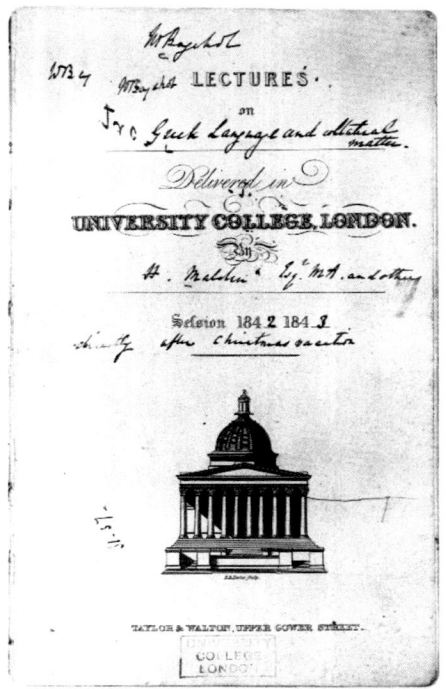

One of Bagehot's notebooks

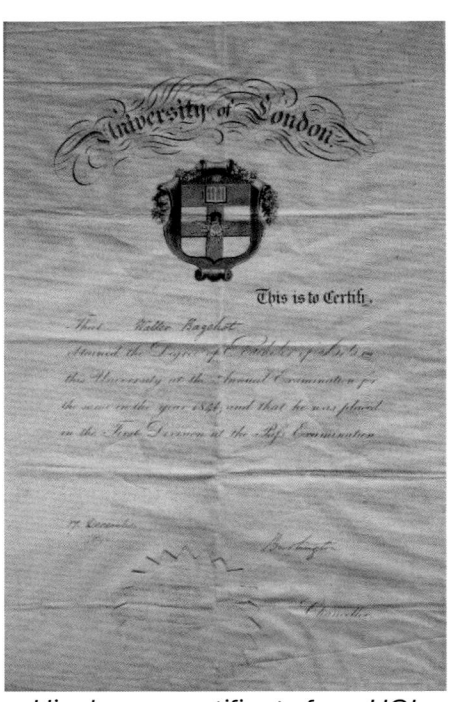

His degree certificate from UCL

He continued to have periods of homesickness and dislike of London. After his exams in June 1846, for example, he was, as usual, downbeat about his performance, and wrote to his father:

> I want to come home exceedingly; for I am so tired of London that I should be g.ad to be out of it on any terms. My dislike of London came on quite suddenly, as it always does, two or three days ago. I know from experience that it will not go off till I have had a run in the country for a short time. I shall, as you know, soon have to come back to bricks and smoke, but this must be endured. I think the people who come up to London 'for the season' must be insane; or they must have different tastes from mine.

Fortunately, despite all these travails, his academic record was exceptional. He came third with first class honours for classics in 1843, writing to his mother: "I have just come back from Somerset House, and beg leave to inform you that, in spite of all croaking and forebodings, I am actually past and in the *first-class*. Also that I have been further recommended to go in for honours both in Classics and Mathematics."

His academic focus was on these two subjects, especially the latter, as he wrote to his father from his lodgings in August 1846:

> I am principally engaged on Pure Mathematics at present, and am going over carefully all the necessary ground - I am going rather slowly perhaps, but I do not wish to leave any enemies in my rear. It is best, of course, to take the Pure Mathematics before the applied, since unless you know a science well applications will certainly be obscure. ... which will be refreshing. I have been reading some of the Theory of Numbers, which De Morgan says is the best exercise for the read possible, and certainly is a hard stretch for my reading powers and memory.

The De Morgan he mentioned was the celebrated Professor of Mathematics, Augustus De Morgan (1806-71), who featured in many of his letters home. He was clearly fascinated by him, even though, he, like most of his fellow students, found the subjects of his lectures very challenging, and he kept copious notes on them in his surviving notebooks. He was clearly eager to engage with the formidable academic, and Hutton later noted how he would ply De Morgan with incisive questions.

Bagehot studying mathematics with Professor De Morgan

In a letter to his mother in October 1842, young Walter described De Morgan thus:

> Professor De Morgan has one eye, and a large white face, rather like Mr. Paul in his manner. He lectures very well, and seems as interested in mathematics, as if he were lecturing on them for the first time, and had not been going continually over the same ground these ten years.

A few weeks later, he ended a letter home, "I must say good-bye as I am scribbling, when I ought to be reading Mr. De Morgan on 'the square roots of unity!'

In 1846 he was again in the first class in 1846 when taking his BA. This latter achievement secured him a scholarship to do postgraduate work for an MA at the University, which allowed him to take his studies to a higher level, and would be helpful if he pursued a career at the Bar. He took new lodgings at 6 Great Coram Street, and achieved his Masters degree in 1848. He was awarded a gold medal for moral and intellectual philosophy (which required him to be helped up by a friend to receive it that summer because of his ill-health). He maintained a close connection with UCL, accepting with delight the offer of becoming a Fellow in 1849, and in the same year he became a 'Proprietor', that is a shareholder, the method used to fund the establishment of the college.

For all the disadvantages of London, the capital did afford Walter the opportunity to be at the centre of political crises and activities. Though parliamentary debates were not accessible because the Palace of Westminster was still being rebuilt after the great fire of 1834, he could and did attend public meetings featuring many of the great orators of the day on the principal political topics such as Richard Cobden and John Bright on the Corn Laws and Free Trade, and Daniel O'Connell on the Irish Question, as well as meetings on slavery, chartism and other liberal reforms.

His London student years certainly matured the teenage Bagehot, both in intellectual thought and his social interactions. At the outset, however, one episode displayed his early priggishness, when he discovered that a couple of his fellow student lodgers at Dr Hoppus' Camden house were spending much of their time with women. After much equivocation, he felt compelled to denounce them to his landlord, and they were dismissed from the lodgings, which did not endear him to his contemporaries.

He was probably never popular with the wider student population, but he did make several close friends who were long-lasting. One was Timothy Smith Osler, whom he had slightly known from Bristol College. Another was William Caldwell Roscoe who, with his even closer and influential friend (and examinations rival) Richard Holt Hutton, were instrumental in reforming UCL's Debating Society. More generally they pursued all sorts of intellectual stimulation, which led him quickly into the world of highbrow magazines and journals, a world he was to inhabit in later years with such renown. The close friendship with Hutton grew as much out of contrasts in their characters as their similarities; they complemented each other to the benefit of both. In addition, he maintained a more long-distance acquaintance with a Bristol College friend, Constantine Prichard, and met through him, the poet Arthur Hugh Clough, with whom he became close in his later student years.

After all this academic success the next stage was a careeer in the law, and he began to take the necessary steps to join the English Bar.

CHAPTER FIVE

Turning point 1: law, letters and Langport

The law student

It had been his father's ambition that Walter would pursue a career in the law, but he himself was probably never keen on this, though he had acquiesced in his father's wishes. So in January 1847 Walter became a member of Lincoln's Inn, judged by the family to be the best of the four Inns of Court, as the first step to becoming a barrister. After gaining his MA, and a summer spent back home at Herd's Hill, Walter duly joined the chambers of Charles Hall in November 1848.

A 19th century photograph of Lincoln's Inn

The following month he described his new life in a letter to his father, in a tone which aimed to be upbeat, but where his antipathy was already showing:

> I am now thoroughly involved in the routine of a law student's life. I go to chambers every day at ten and return at five with exemplary regularity. While I am there, I read law and copy precedents, or read the cases that are sent into the pupil room or draw any paper that is easy and that Mr. Hall deems suitable to my uninitiated mind ... I find the work rather fatiguing at present. My eye is not practised enough to see easily the contents of a law paper. I do not know what are the material and what the immaterial parts; and groping all through masses of papers is a tiring operation, and a capital way of picking up a headache. I am I hope however already acquiring more facility than I had at first. But the progress is slow, and the process of learning this part of the subject not the most agreeable. Reading law treatises however is much easier and pleasanter.

Within a short time, he was keen to move on to another chambers dealing with different areas of law, but his arguments for this shift did not initially meet with his father's approval, and he had to push hard to make the move to the chambers of J R Quain. There, despite some breaks, he persevered in his 'apprenticeship', and completed the various arcane requirements, such as 'eating dinners', and was called to the Bar in November 1852. Bagehot channelled his negative experience of his legal education to good use in a scathing June 1870 *Fortnightly Review* article, entitled 'Bad lawyers or good?' on the subject of its reform.

The time had come for Walter to decide whether to pursue a law career or change course. His mother had long suggested he return home and work in the family businesses, ostensibly out of concern for his health, but more likely because she wanted him close to help look after her and the family. In letters as far back as the spring of 1845, she had urged him to consider such an option (perhaps prompted further by the death that May of her brother, Vincent Stuckey, the undisputed head of the family businesses):

> But turn your attention a little to business when you are at home, try to understand Papa's cleverness in it, and if very or totally inferior at first, do not be depressed. If he were to die now, which God forbid! I am sure I should at once wish you to *understand what business is*. I have often told dearest Papa, it was a fault more of his habits than his intentions, that he had not, as a matter of course, made you better acquainted with its practical details and mysteries

He had clearly been discussing his future with his father, not just in terms of his wish to be a lawyer or not, but also in relation to being a support to the family, especially his mother, whose health was fragile. Throughout this unhappy time in London, he was determined to put on a positive front to his mother, who worried about his health and prospects. This is best demonstrated by an amusing and upbeat letter to her in May 1851 describing his attendance at the opening by the Queen of the Great Exhibition in Hyde Park, which included this typical Bagehotian gem: "The only accurate idea that I can give you of the Exhibition is that it is a great fair under a cucumber frame." In passing, it may be noted from a letter to his friend Hutton that June that he may have gone to it often, as so many people did, though in a more active capacity than most: "I stand & give lectures on lady's dress and furniture & machinery with admirable pluck & much emphasis."

He had a number of options to consider, including a temporary if indeterminate move back to Langport (whether or not that involved him working in the bank or other family businesses in some capacity), with a possible return thereafter to London and the law. He could even, as appears from this correspondence with his father, have been considering combining the two in some way, but this was seen as impractical. As an unusual foretaste, in March 1851, while still at his legal training, he had been asked to research an obscure point of ecclesiastical law for the Bank regarding a troubled £1,000 loan to a Kingsbury church.

His own views of the relative merits of living in Langport or London had oscillated. Despite his antipathy to much of what London meant, he recognised the many advantages it could have for him - especially if he had any thoughts of becoming some sort of writer. Given his intellectual and educational achievements, writing in some form, whether professionally or largely recreationally, would have been an obvious consideration. The consistent encouragement of his parents in his rigorous education suggests that they may well have supported some literary activity by young Walter. London, with its access to the 'corridors of power' and the existing print and publishing media, would be a convenient base for such literary pursuits, and this latter view became clearer to him when he was in rural Somerset.

Back in Langport in the spring of 1851, he wrote to his friend, Roscoe that he had "settled to go into equity. I couldn't live cheerfully down here, and though I regret immensely that I ever opened a law book, I must stick to London now come what may, and I am sure of enough to live on, in any case."

According to Hutton, he felt unsuited to the life of a working barrister, partly on health grounds, "he was sure that his head would not stand the hot Courts and heavy wigs which make the hot Courts hotter, or the night-work of a thriving barrister in case of success; and he was certainly quite right."

Following his eventful Paris sojourn in 1851-2 (discussed below), he came to a definite conclusion, which he confirmed in letters from London to his father in August 1852, though he couched it overtly in terms of his possible law career, rather than more domestic reasons:

> I have been considering carefully the question which we almost decided upon when I was at home - I mean my abandoning the law at the present crisis - and in accordance with what we very nearly resolved. upon when I was with you. I have decided to do so at this juncture utterly and for ever. ... I am reluctant, I own to do this as I like law, and have spent a good deal of time upon it, and if I thought that my chances of success were reasonably sure I should still - go on - but I do not think so - on the contrary imagine that 'under all circumstances' the common sense is to leave it and therefore I do leave it. What I mean to do in other pursuits, must be entirely decided by what it is found I can do, when I am tried in them, but I assume that we quite resolved on the first step - that I should go into the counting house and remain there under your direction until I am decently fit to go elsewhere. And this is all which need be stated in this letter.

In a follow-up letter a couple of weeks later, he expanded on this decision and its consequences:

> My love to my mother. I hope she will support my change of plans with Equanimity, if you have announced it to her. ... I confess also that I doubt if it would have been possible to try business adequately, without such an absence from law as would be equivalent to abandoning it, but we need scarcely now discuss this. As to what you say of business itself, I hope I shall always be ready to do my best - though I certainly do not imagine that I shall set the Parret on fire, at any rate not immediately.

Letters from Paris

Opportunities to write soon arose. The first was the chance to contribute three articles to a quarterly journal, the *Prospective Review*, in 1847-48, while he was still doing his postgraduate work. They were on very different topics, beginning with a review of *Festus*, a very long poem based on the Faustian myth, in November 1847. This was followed by 'The currency monopoly' the following August, and a review three months later, of John Stuart Mill's *Principles of Political Economy*. That a young student, barely into his twenties, was able to be published at all, never mind with three substantial pieces in a year, may have had something to do with several of his friends, including Hutton and Roscoe, being involved with the journal.

However, none of this, impressive as it was, was likely to propel Bagehot to literary celebrity. What did give him some unexpected early recognition, even notoriety, was the result of a fortuitous coincidence, arising out of his indecision and anxiety about his professional future following his legal studies, a couple of years later.

It was suggested to him – probably by his friend Roscoe, as a January 1852 letter from Walter to him implies – that he should take a holiday in France, and so in August 1851 he went to Paris. The notional reason for the trip was the improvement of his French, but clearly a complete break would do him good. He stayed with a family called Bein at Rue de Vangirard. He met up with a Mme Meynieux, who was a friend of his mother and he also befriended Mme Mohl, whose salon hosted many society notables.

More surprisingly, he took up waltzing, or at least a variation of it, as he admitted to his mother in a letter in late December 1851: "It differs from what other people call by that name, not only in the step which is of my own invention, but also in its having no relation whatever to the music, and by preserving its rotator motion in a great measure by collisions with other couples. It's very amusing running small French girls against some fellow's elbow, it's like killing flies years ago."

Clearly the trip was having a positive effect on Walter. He confessed, in a January 1852 letter to Roscoe, that "I was very unwell mentally and bodily when I came here. I had a good deal to put me out. Everything of all kinds had gone wrong with me for a long time, and there were some family matters which much annoyed me besides, so I was in a very weak-minded state." It was not only the social whirl that refreshed him. It was a political coup.

A French Deputy at the barricades during the coup of December 1851

Louis Napoleon, nephew of Bonaparte himself, was President of France, but under the existing constitution he could not be re-elected. On 2 December he staged an audacious *coup d'etat* - including the dissolution of the Legislative Assembly and the arrest of around 20,000 potential opponents - to retain power, despite determined but short-lived opposition from dissident Republicans, who erected barricades in Paris.

Walter had explained what he described as "an interesting crisis in politics here just now" in a letter to his mother in October. The coup energised Walter, who realised that he had a front row seat to a major political crisis, and he regaled his mother and friends with what amounted to 'war correspondent' reports.

More importantly, he had seven 'letters' on the French situation published between January and March in the *Inquirer* (another journal in which his friends were involved), his first published work since 1848. Though they were signed 'Amicus', his true identity was soon known. Their animated tone and their political line generally in favour of the coup because he thought it would bring stability, were rather daring for a young amateur journalist, and hardly in line with British opinion. Despite this considered pro-Napoleon line, he was so swept up in the sheer excitement and chaos, that he even assisted in constructing the barricades of the dissident Republicans.

Though it would be an exaggeration to claim that the *Inquirer* articles made his reputation, it did confirm to his own satisfaction that he had genuine writing skills, and this transformed his mental state. It made easier his decision to leave the law and to return to Langport, where a less-pressured lifestyle could afford him time and space to continue writing.

The young Langport banker – and writer

So Walter swapped metropolitan London and the Bar for rural Langport and a life of business. As agreed with his father, he worked in Stuckey's Bank while he considered his more long-term options. With his father being so senior in the Bank, it seems that Bagehot's initial position there was akin to what may nowadays be termed a 'nepo intern', as it is unclear whether he was actually employed or paid then.

As early as October 1852, he was writing to Arthur Hugh Clough, explaining this major career shift: "I have changed my own plans in life since I saw you last. I have given up law, and taken to banking and gone into trade. I do not think that I shall like it so well as I shd. have liked law, if I had seen a reasonable certainty of speedy or even eventual employment, but I did not see any in the existing confusion of the profession - and I possess connections and advantages here which make the mercantile alternative a reasonable certainty."

Despite what may have been early misgivings about this major move in his life, he came to understand and even enjoy it. From Langport, he wrote to his friends in somewhat wry terms about his new life. In a letter of January 1853 to an old school-friend, Killigrew Wait, he described being a novice country banker:

> Here am I in my father's counting-house trying (and failing) to do sums, and being rowed ninety-nine times a day for some horrid sin against the conventions of mercantile existence. My family perhaps you know are merchants, shipowners, and bankers, &c. &c., here and elsewhere. Out of their multifarious occupations I hope to be able to find, though I cannot precisely say that I have yet found, some one to which I am not contemptibly unequal. ... The only thing I ever really knew was Special Pleading, and the moment I had learned that, the law reformers botched and abolished it ... I suppose you like business

by this time. I think I might if I knew anything about it, and if my relations would admit that sums are matters of opinion.

In similar terms, he wrote to his friend, Hutton the same month:

> I have devoted my time for the last four months nearly exclusively to the art of book-keeping by double entry, the theory of which is agreeable and pretty but the practice perhaps as horrible as anything ever was. …. In other respects I approve of mercantile life. There is some excitement in it, if this does not wear off; always a little to do and no wearing labour, which is something towards perfection.

Though he described rural life after London in the same letter as "stupefying … one gets into a rut of ideas and society, the same since our grandfathers fell asleep, from which living tomb nothing after a short time will ever save one," it allowed him to assist his family, especially his increasingly unwell mother; enabled him to indulge his passions of riding and hunting, and it also gave him more opportunities to write.

He did have to juggle his new banking duties with his writing, as he indicated with a weary sigh in a letter to his friend Roscoe in March 1853: "I will arrange about the Prospective [Review] though what to write about I know no more than the people in the street. I write with ever so many people talking figures about me and I hardly know what I write."

His trial period in the 'counting house' must have been successful in the eyes of both himself and his father, because, at a meeting of the Stuckey's Bank Directors at Taunton on Saturday 18 June 1853, as recorded in the Minutes, his father got the Directors' agreement to Walter working more formally in the Bank: "Mr Bagehot having requested that his son Mr Walter Bagehot might be allowed to attend at the Bank in Langport, with a view to his making himself acquainted with the Business, his wish was acceded to."

Reflecting on Walter's business relationship with his father in her 1914 biography of him, Emilie Barrington noted the great contrast between the solemnity of the father, who regarded all aspects of business as a very serious and meticulous matter, with the more carefree and relaxed attitudes of the son. Despite this, Mr Bagehot appreciated the value and utility of his son's unique approach and he "gradually learnt to lean on his judgment and opinions."

Walter quickly rose in the ranks of the Langport businesses (including the shipping and mercantile aspects), evidently on merit rather than through his family connections. In October 1855, he was appointed Secretary to the Stuckey's Bank Committees of Management, Langport & Bristol, at a salary of £200 a year, and became a director in the following year.

In Somerset, Walter did not spend all his time on business. On his return from Paris, he still wrote for the *Inquirer* and the *Prospective Review*, and this continued apace after the move to Langport. This included some of his best work, like his essay on Shakespeare in 1853. On that front, his main focus in the mid-1850s was the establishment of the *National Review*. Running and writing for this journal occupied much of his time right through until 1864.

He and Hutton founded this new journal to replace the sinking *Prospective Review*. He not only contributed many of its articles (at the same time he also wrote frequently for the *Saturday Review*), but also arranged its finances, production and editorial line over the decade of its existence. The surviving correspondence of the period shows in quite some detail the trials and tribulations Bagehot and his group endured in getting this ambitious project off the ground.

As was common in those days, serious publications of this sort tended to issue a 'prospectus', stating its proposed aims and philosophy, to attract financial backers, potential contributors and readers. From an internal perspective, the very process of producing such a manifesto would enable the proposed founders to thrash out any potential differences of opinion amongst them – including the tricky but crucial issue of the publication's title - and to ensure, as far as practicable, a united approach. A draft prospectus was prepared, and a final version issued in 1855.

The first issues were published in mid-1855, and under the editorship of Bagehot and Hutton the new journal gradually gained a small but growing circulation both in the UK and the USA, but the American Civil War dented this progress. When Hutton resigned the editorship in 1862, as did his successor shortly thereafter, Walter assumed the full editorial burden. However, falling circulation and the withdrawal of external financial support due to differences over the Review's theological stance made it increasingly unviable, and it folded in 1864.

The *National Review* was a convenient outlet for his writing, especially of a non-economic nature. Most of his contributions were on literary subjects from Milton, Scott, Dickens and Thackeray to Wordsworth, Browning and Tennyson, and on current and historical political figures such as Bolingbroke, Pitt, Peel, and Gladstone. Some of his best and most influential work appeared in it, including the important career-boosting article on parliamentary reform in January 1859. It also provided him with invaluable experience in all aspects of running a publication, which stood him in good stead when he took over *The Economist*.

This dual life as banker and writer seemed set to be his not unhappy lot for the future. But the latter 1850s brought further unexpected and life-changing developments.

CHAPTER SIX

Bagehot in business

All these momentous changes began Bagehot's final period of working mainly in the world of trade and commerce. Until he started writing for *The Economist* in the late 1850s, this world was largely that of the family's banking and mercantile businesses in Somerset. How did Bagehot adjust to these new horizons?

Many of Bagehot's writings, especially those of an economic nature, were written with what he called 'men of business' in mind. His 1873 'Wilson Memorandum' on *The Economist* explicitly states that "The politics of the paper must be viewed mainly with reference to the tastes of men of business. It is among them and among them only that the Economist will ever circulate ..."

Was Bagehot himself such a 'man of business'? Could he understand their concerns and write about them with empathy and experience, especially in *The Economist* or in his works on finance? In reality his direct business experience was limited in the context of the rapidly industrialising economy of Victorian Britain. He was not himself a captain of industry, or what we would think of as an entrepreneur or venture capitalist, and would have mainly encountered that world either as clients of the Bank or socially.

Nevertheless, he did seem to have an affinity with the 'man of business', as the growing success of *The Economist* and his other financial works were to demonstrate, and he often wrote about matters from their perspective. He would have followed the business careers of his family, especially his father's, and would have appreciated the material and social benefits such commercial prosperity brought. He might possibly have returned to his merchant roots after his academic and legal education in any case, even if there had not been compelling family reasons and pressures to abandon a nascent career at the Bar in 1852.

As has been seen, after initially struggling with his new banking job in Langport, he quickly developed an aptitude for it and even began to enjoy the commercial life. His friends and family often quoted him as saying throughout the rest of his life that 'business is much more amusing than pleasure' (the exact quote varies with recollection). This chapter will take forward this aspect of his life, both in the family businesses and in other ways, other than the running of *The Economist* itself.

Country banker

His steady rise in Stuckey's Bank through the mid-1850s was significantly affected by the association, both professional and personal, with the Wilson family. His marriage to Eliza Wilson in 1858 and his growing involvement with James Wilson's paper, *The Economist*, especially after the latter's unexpected death in India in late 1860, meant that his banking career would no longer be so 'hands-on', based in Langport, but of a more supervisory, executive nature from his new permanent base in London. The profound Wilson impact on his life and career is discussed in the following chapter.

Whether or not, or to what extent, his rise in the Bank was due to his family connections – it would not be fanciful to assume that Walter's father, in particular, should wish to see the Bagehot presence continue after his own retirement from the upper echelons of the Bank's management – it must be that Walter's own abilities and personality reinforced such promotion. If he had not proved himself to be such an asset, nepotism would surely only have taken him so far, and he might well have been shunted aside to some obscure but comfortable post, away from any front line responsibilities.

From his initial introduction in late 1852 as a kind of 'intern', through his gradual adoption of more responsible duties, Walter was, by 1855, both a shareholder (he was granted 26 shares on 29 January) and Secretary to the newly established Committee of Management (he was appointed on 22 October, with a salary of £200 a year). The following year, he was appointed as Secretary to the Directors, and in 1858, after his marriage, he was given more responsibilities in the Bank generally, and in the management of the Bristol branch in particular. By the end of that year, he was co-manager at Bristol, working 3 days there, and 2 days at Langport, with a substantially increased salary of £500 a year, with a shareholding of 30 shares.

Walter Bagehot's travelling briefcase, ideal for the busy commuter

The impact of the Wilsons on his banking career began to be felt even more strongly when James Wilson's departure to India in late 1859, and Bagehot's assumption of a more senior role with *The Economist,* necessitated significant changes to his work patterns. He wrote to the Bank informing them of his new situation, "which might interfere with the arrangement made with the bank two years ago". He said that his attendance at Bristol would be the same, but he wouldn't be able to be at Langport so often. The Directors, mindful of the potential value of his new London position (and of his family connections in the Bank, no doubt), were keen to retain his services, albeit in a revised capacity. On 14 December they resolved that, as his attendance at Bristol would be the same, and because "his attention to the financial business of the company in London is very desirable", no change in remuneration would be necessary.

This did not remain a stable arrangement for long. When Wilson died in India in 1860, even greater London-based responsibilities fell on Bagehot's relatively young shoulders. On 11 February 1861 Bagehot wrote to the Directors asking that he be allowed to reside in London and that the times of his attendance at Bristol be altered. His father put his case to a Bank meeting on 13 February, but a decision was postponed.

At their next meeting on 13 March, the Directors were 'of the opinion' that: Bagehot should resign local managership of the Bristol bank; continue to be Secretary to the Committee and Directors; his attention should be considerably directed to the superintending at the Bristol bank; he should agree with the Committee the modes and times of his superintendence, which should be substantial and not nominal; as he had offered to help them invest their surplus London money, he should gain and give them all the information in his power respecting the money market, the actual investment of the money being left to the Committee, and his residence in London should not entail any additional expenses on the Bank. His new salary would be £300 a year.

That effectively settled Bagehot's banking career for the rest of his life. He would attend major Bank meetings, whether of Directors or shareholders ('proprietors') in Langport or in other locations around Somerset; he would have some residual duties in Bristol, and he would be the Bank's 'eyes and ears' in London gleaning news and opinion relevant to the Bank's business interests.

His status and stake in the Bank, nevertheless, continued to grow. In July 1864 he was elected a Director of the Bank, and in April 1868 he was added to the Committee of Management as an unpaid member, but without the obligation to attend constantly. A Directors' meeting in Bridgwater on 25 January 1876 confirmed his election as its Vice Chairman (the highest position his father had attained).

In March 1866 his salary was increased from £300 a year to £400 a year, and his shareholding grew. He had ˄30 shares by May 1867 (presumably including the Wilson shares), which his recent biographer, James Grant, calculated as being at that stage, 45 more than his father, and 3.4% of the 3830 outstanding issued shares. By July 1874 he had 143 shares. As well as giving him a stake in the Company, the generous and ever-growing dividends paid on Stuckey Bank shares also provided him with a very decent income, earning him more than many senior Bank clerks earned in salary.

As to his bank duties and activities from the early 1860s until his death in 1877, Bank archives, surviving correspondence and Eliza's diaries attest to his diligence. Virtually every fortnight he would travel to Somerset to attend bank meetings (and, of course, to visit family and friends in and around Langport). Often he would travel alone, leaving Eliza in London, which could cause friction, as when she complained in her diary on 21 April 1869 that he had missed their anniversary by attending a meeting at Taunton that very day (the entry ended, "in bed all day.") Even when on personal visits to Langport, Bank-related events would occur, such as hosting regular 'bankers' dinners' at Herd's Hill, for senior Bank staff and other local worthies.

He sometimes had to deal with West Country issues, such as in July 1869 when he went to Bristol by the morning express and "took down young Mr Deedes, on trial as a new additional manager at the bank there." The diary also records in late 1872, Bagehot having settled 'l'affaire Badcock', which may have been an oblique reference to the Stuckey takeover of the Badcock Bank of Taunton (a matter which also required a later visit to Exeter from Langport by Bagehot, not returning home to London until 11pm).

Examples of his London bank activities include a report he made to a Bank committee meeting in November 1861 on the value of their American securities. In March 1865, he was requested by the Bank to attend a meeting of a committee made up of various banks of issue which was monitoring a parliamentary bill going through the House of Commons which affected them. He reported back to a meeting on 29 March, with news of the Government's latest position on the bill.

Bank House, the original Stuckey's Bank building

There must have been many other instances over these years when Bagehot would have fed the Bank information or other titbits of interest gleaned from what would have been meetings, events and the like in which he may have participated primarily in a different capacity, such as editor of *The Economist* or even as a friend and acquaintance at a social function. His multiple roles in London, and the 'insider' status he acquired, must have inevitably led to what would now be thought of as conflicts of interests and similar ethical concerns. He would often make a case to officials or politicians, using his Stuckey's experience as an illustration, though he would be at pains to say, in appropriate cases, that he was not offering any advice on their behalf.

However too much can be made of his presumed status in London as a banker. He was certainly not as influential as his uncle Vincent Stuckey, who *was* the Bank in decades past. Bagehot was not the head of the Bank, and the Bank itself, for all its size, prestige and profitability, was still merely a provincial banking group based in the West Country. Such clout as Bagehot possessed in the financial and political corridors of power derived not from his banking position, but from his editorship of *The Economist* and from his wider writings.

Perhaps he sometimes yearned to be a big London banker, like some of his friends and acquaintances. His *Lombard Street* descriptions of the lives of successful bankers in the money markets and financial houses in the City paint a rather rosy picture of not too laborious a life, with plenty of time for other pursuits, intellectual or otherwise. "There has probably very rarely ever been so happy a position as that of a London private banker; and never perhaps a happier."

Other family businesses

While a fair amount is known of Bagehot as a banker and as a writer and editor, relatively little detail is available of his participation in the other family businesses in Langport and around Somerset. The main sources, such as correspondence, archives and diaries allude to his involvement but do not indicate how active he was.

Part of the reason for this is that during his career as a country banker with Stuckey's, that Bank would have been the principal, if not the only bank for the family businesses and their associated enterprises. Just as, in the beginning, the Bank grew out of, and as adjunct to these existing mercantile businesses, this muddied the waters about the capacity in which he may have been acting at any particular time. A related aspect is the relative fluidity and inter-connectedness between these various businesses. In the days before comprehensive company registration, when partnerships and other forms of business relationship were often relatively informal, and subject to frequent changes of personnel and name, confident identification of particular enterprises at particular points in time is not always possible.

The main business was that of Stuckey & Bagehot, founded sometime after 1747, and consisting over time of various combinations of members of the two families. By the time of Bagehot's childhood the main players included his uncle Vincent Stuckey (head of the Bank) and Thomas Watson Bagehot, his father, and its main business was the Parrett river trade, based at what is now Great Bow Wharf, by the main Langport bridge and high street. Other combinations of the two families, together with other partners traded in the goods that were shipped along the Parrett, such as coal and salt, the latter being a major and lucrative Stuckey-led enterprise.

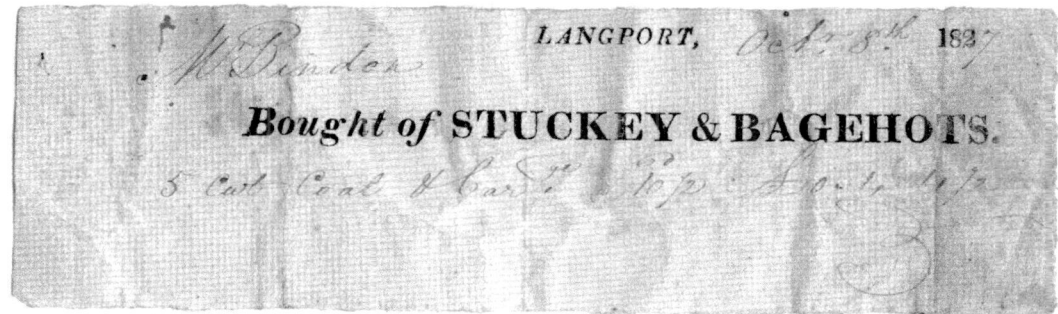

A receipt dated 8 October 1827, for 5 cwt of coal, plus carriage, costing £10-5 shillings

In 1855 Stuckey & Bagehot hived off their coal and timber businesses to Edward Bagehot (Walter Bagehot's uncle) and Watson Bagehot (his cousin), and this became known as E&W Bagehot, with Stuckey & Bagehot focussing on their water-related businesses. In 1862, E&W Bagehot was renamed the Somerset Trading Company, which expanded, after Walter's death, into the Bridgwater brick and tile trade.

Alongside the core family enterprises were others in which they, as individuals or as the above-named enterprises, were involved. The most relevant of these was the Parrett Navigation Company, established in 1836 by Private Act of Parliament (and with increased powers in a further Act in 1839), to improve the decaying infrastructure of the River Parrett (such as by building a new, improved Langport bridge), to stave off threats to their activities from new canals and other schemes for trade to bypass Langport entirely. No less a figure than Isambard Kingdom Brunel had come to Langport and advised on these proposals, though he was not directly involved in their later design or construction.

Like Stuckey's Bank, which became a joint-stock company, and then a limited liability company under relevant legislation, the Parrett Navigation Company was a legal entity, distinct from his major owners, such as Stuckey & Bagehot and other interested local businesses. Stuckey & Bagehot were initially opposed to the proposed new enterprise for fear that it would undermine its existing privileged position in the river trade, but eventually came on board as a major player, through the participation of Thomas Watson Bagehot and Vincent Stuckey.

The Parrett Navigation Company was profitable for a while, due to the improvements they had made, but it suffered a mortal blow with the coming of the railways, especially with a station opening in 1853 diagonally across the river from Great Bow Wharf, at what is now the Westover Trading Estate. By mid-1877, its position was hopeless, with the river trade virtually wiped out and the costs of its maintenance of the Navigation becoming ever more uneconomic. It was dissolved in 1878 and its Navigation functions transferred to a new statutory body, the Somerset Drainage Commissioners. Ironically this period of decline almost exactly mirrors the entire span of Walter Bagehot's working life.

Bagehot would have grown up in an environment dominated by his father's and his wider family's banking activities, and their other mercantile enterprises, such as the Parrett river trade. The Stuckeys and the Bagehots were the two dominant commercial families in the Langport of his youth, and influential in the wider economy in their part of Somerset, and he would have absorbed that atmosphere, even if not necessarily every detail of their daily activities. In 1869, speaking largely from a Bridgwater focus, he described his mercantile background: "I am director of Stuckey's bank, and am connected with this borough in this way, that my family have been traders for a very considerable period; 70 years or somewhere about that I should think. They are not largely interested in the trade now, but still they have some connexion with it, and my father lives near. I am connected with the neighbourhood."

There are examples of his apparent interest in his childhood letters, as has been seen, for example, first in a letter written to a Bridgwater relative, probably in 1831, when he would have been only 4 or 5, asking about progress in the building of one of the business's ships, the *Britannia*, and secondly, his 1839 letter to his father about a boatmen's strike.

Bagehot himself alluded obliquely to involvement in these activities, at least in the early days, through his work at the Bank. For example, in a March 1855 letter to his friend, Hutton, about the setting-up and editorship of the proposed *National Review*, he wrote:

> Even if it were offered me I could not have the responsibility of the Review absolutely on me. It wd. be sure to come at a time when there was a press of work in banking or shipping, and either the no. wd. not appear - if it did appear it wd. be certainly misprinted - or I must neglect what I have undertaken here, which I shd. of course not choose to do.

All of this experience fed into his professional writing. In an 1860 article, "The Merchant's Function" he could opine, with confidence, that "[t]he only sound and practical view is that ... the very desire and efforts of the merchant to make money will be the best security for the due discharge of his function and secure the amplest provision for the community."

What is lacking in the record is the detail of his day-to-day involvement in these mercantile businesses, especially in the 1850s and 1860s. Commentators and biographers have had to resort to creative imaginings of this aspect of his life, as did Woodrow Wilson: "His father was interested in large commercial undertakings, and was a ship-owner as well as a banker, and his son found, in association with him, an active enough life, full of travel and of important errands here and there, upon which he could spend his energies with not a little satisfaction."

Emilie Barrington, who would have had greater direct knowledge through her own observation and access to her sister Eliza's diaries, wrote in similar vein, referring, as did her sister, to the various family and related mercantile enterprises as 'the Bridge business' (alluding to their HQ at Great Bow Wharf being adjacent to Langport bridge). Interestingly, Vincent Stuckey in his 1844 will (he died the following year) used a similar term when he referred to his capital in, and the profits, buildings and other property of "the trade at Langport called 'The Bridge Trade'".

An early view of Great Bow Bridge over the River Parrett with Great Bow Wharf beyond it

She discussed how Walter would have taken to these more practical activities. "At the Bank or at The Bridge no speculations on the mysteries and puzzles of life could invade and take possession, no leaps or flights of imagination could interfere with business. ... the Bank and The Bridge gradually became interesting."

The existing Eliza Bagehot diaries lack a number of the relevant years of Bagehot's business life, but those that do survive suggest a level of involvement in his later years in the mercantile businesses as more of a supervisory, advisory role (often doubtless with his Bank hat on), rather than a more hands-on basis. Some examples will provide a flavour. There are regular references to his attendance at meetings of these businesses, perhaps even as a shareholder/proprietor/partner. In late March 1875 he was involved in discussions about the Parrett Navigation Company, and, in particular, problems with closing the Langport lock on the river for drainage purposes. In mid-May that year, Watson Bagehot saw him at Herd's Hill to talk about business, and later the same day Edward Bagehot arrived and "had a long talk with Walter about the bridge business." Most poignantly, on 22 March 1877, when Walter was on his death-bed, "Watson B[agehot] & Barnes B[agehot] saw W about the Bridge meeting while it was going on."

Other evidence of Walter's mercantile activity includes his becoming an insurance underwriter at Lloyds of London in 1856, though Robert Giffen, his colleague at *The Economist*, claimed that he took "no part, however, in the active detailed business, which was done for him by proxy." Whether this was associated with his roles in the family business, or was more in the nature of a personal investment, is not known.

He did write wryly once, from such indirect knowledge, about underwriting, in an 1866 article on the little Cornish port of Boscastle:

> I suppose we ought to think much of the courage with which sailors face such dangers, and of the feelings of their wives and families when they wait the return of their husbands and fathers; but my City associations at once carried me away to the poor underwriter who should insure against loss at such a place. How he would murmur, 'Oh! my premium,' as he saw the ship tossing up to the great black rock and the ugly breakwater, and seeming likely enough to hit both. I shall not ask at Lloyds' what is the rate for Boscastle rocks, for I remember the grave rebuke I once got from a serious underwriter when I said some other such place was pretty. 'Pretty! I should think it was' he answered; 'why it is lined with our money!'

He was also a director of the British Shipowners Company of Liverpool from its creation in 1864 until 1871. He is listed in the details of the directors in newspaper notices of 1864 as "Walter Bagehot Esq, Messrs Stuckey and Bagehot, Langport and Stuckey's Bank Company, Langport and Bristol." His trip to Liverpool in late March 1864 was noted in his wife Eliza's diary: "He went to Liverpool to attend a meeting of the proposed ship company of which he is to be a director."

He had shares in at least 5 ocean-going ships, though the relevant ownership records show that most of his holdings were on behalf of Stuckey & Bagehot.

He is also recorded as holding shares in the Great Western Railway, in a joint account with his wife's uncle George Wilson, which may relate to a minute in the Bank records of Aug 1873, approving a loan of £5000 to Bagehot and Wilson. This may have been a personal matter, as it has been suggested that Wilson was in financial difficulties at that time, or it may relate to them being co-executors of James Wilson's estate.

Finally, there is a reference in Eliza Bagehot's will to a holding of Somersetshire Trading Company shares. As she died in 1921, more than four decades after her husband's death, this may have related to a period during her widowhood, rather than something inherited from Walter or another Bagehot family member.

His recent biographer, James Grant states clearly that "his only known investment was Stuckey's Banking Company." If this is the case in terms of personal, private holdings, this suggests that any other investments, such as those just listed, were likely to be related, in some way, to his professional involvement in the family businesses or in his legal capacity as a trustee and executor.

For many men of Bagehot's time and class, the activities described here would probably have amounted to a full and active professional life. That he did all this, as well as his banking and writing/editing, despite persistent poor health, is a testament to his extraordinary commitment, stamina and energy.

The refurbished Great Bow Wharf, Bow Street, Langport

CHAPTER SEVEN

Turning point 2: Eliza and The Economist

A meeting at Claverton Manor

In December 1856, William Rathbone Greg, of *The Economist*, approached Richard Holt Hutton to ask if he would be interested in becoming its editor. Hutton was keen, but planned to be abroad for some time to visit his late wife's tomb in the West Indies. A friend of Bagehot's since university, he sought his advice, and received a clear reply not to miss out on such a plum offer, in Walter's scornful phrase, "for the sake of *holiday*." To ram the point home, he added, "Offers of this kind are not to be picked up in the street every day." When Hutton apparently took this advice, Walter was pleased and relieved, assuring his friend that he would improve *The Economist*.

This exchange had piqued Bagehot's interest in offering himself as a contributor to *The Economist*. Perhaps he thought that, as with his earlier published offerings, being a close friend of the incoming editor would do him no harm. He would have been familiar with *The Economist* as a reader from his student days, and he had even written, in somewhat mixed terms, about its proprietor, James Wilson, in a very early published article in the *Prospective Review* in 1848. He mostly praised Wilson's views while criticising the uncorrected inaccuracies in the pamphlet he was reviewing which was based on a series of articles in *The Economist*.

James Wilson, Walter's father-in-law, founder of The Economist

Through intermediaries, including Greg, it was arranged that he would visit Wilson at his rented country home, Claverton Manor, just outside Bath, in January 1857. This meeting turned out to be life-changing for Walter both professionally and personally. Wilson was not only a senior Liberal MP (elected in 1847), and a government minister, but he was also successful in business, and an active journalist and writer. He founded *The Economist* in 1843 and had run it ever since.

From a professional perspective, the Claverton meeting was a success and Walter was commissioned to write a series of twelve 'letters' on banking and currency by 'A Banker', which ran from the 7 February issue until April 1858. Lord Radnor, a political mentor of Wilson, who had helped him found *The Economist*, wrote a tongue-in-cheek letter to Bagehot the day after publication of the first piece, 'The General Aspect of the Banking Question', analysing 'A Banker's' views and suggesting matters he should deal with in future letters.

Thus began Bagehot's association with *The Economist*, initially under the patronage of Wilson and the editorship of Hutton. Other more substantial articles followed, while he continued to write also for the *National Review* and the *Saturday Review*.

Eliza Wilson

Walter first met Elizabeth (Eliza) Wilson on Saturday 24 January 1857 at Claverton Manor, during that pivotal trip. Eliza, then aged 24, was the eldest of six sisters, and Walter took her down to dinner that evening. The remaining sisters saw him for the first time at breakfast the following morning, but Eliza was absent due to a headache. They all seemed to take to him immediately, especially Eliza, and the feeling was mutual. He became like the brother they never had.

Walter and Eliza's courtship proceeded apace during the following months, at Claverton (where Walter stayed at Easter) and at the Wilsons' London residence, 15 Hertford Street, Mayfair. 'Mr Bagehot' increasingly populated Eliza's diary entries, and the relationship grew more serious in the autumn. On 27 September, Walter felt able to tell Eliza of his mother's mental illness, but, fortunately, that did not put Eliza off.

He became an intimate member of the Wilson circle, both through the connection at *The Economist* and his growing connection with Eliza. His life was fast broadening on several fronts, and two contrasting diary glimpses of Walter in 1857 reveal something of his relative social and professional status, especially in London and in Langport, at that time of great transition.

An American friend of Greg's, George Ticknor, attended a small dinner party at the Wilsons' Mayfair home in early July. After remarking on the character of James himself and noting his "young wife and three, nice grown up daughters" – including the eldest, Eliza – he mentions "a barrister – whose name I did not get", who was, of course, Walter. To be so casually misdescribed and passed over, suggests that his metropolitan fame was not that widespread in mid-1857.

However, a month later, another diary, that of the future novelist, Anne Beale (1815-1900), who hailed from Portfield, almost opposite Herd's Hill, suggested how Walter was then viewed in his home town. When she was on a nostalgic visit to Langport in

1857 to meet friends, including the Stuckeys and the Bagehots, Mrs Bagehot had invited her to dinner on 6 August to meet her husband and son. The latter was described in her diary as "a clever writer in the National Review." At the dinner at Herd's Hill, she "was introduced to Mr. Walter Bagehot, the only son, and a genius. I never saw such eyes in my life. Large, wild, fiery, black, clever, and quite strange enough to make anyone fear his mother's unhappy malady in him. He himself very strange also, but as amusing and original as possible. I passed a delightful evening."

It is interesting to note in passing, from Eliza's diary entry of 28 October 1869, that when both she and Walter's mother were unwell at Herd's Hill, "we had some of Miss Beale's new novel *Country courtships* read aloud evening." This presumably indicates that she would have known about the author's Langport roots, and friendships.

Bagehot's intentions towards Eliza were becoming clearer. At the start of November 1857 he had talks with Eliza's parents at Claverton which presumably won their approval of him as a potential son-in-law. Shortly afterwards Walter engineered a chance meeting in the library at Claverton where he proposed to her on Wednesday 4 November. As Eliza's diary put it: "then he got me in here alone under pretence of looking for a book..." It was agreed that she should give her answer when they were back in London. He was not kept waiting for long. On the morning of Saturday the 7th, as Eliza's diary records: "Mr. Bagehot came at 10 for my answer. I was in the dining room, and engaged myself to him then and there ..."

Eliza in 1858

At this crucial point, the couple had to part ways for a time. Walter needed to return to pressing bank business in Langport and in London. Eliza and her younger sister Sophie accompanied their father to Edinburgh, where he had government business. While there, she was due to consult a noted doctor, John Beveridge, who did head massages to cure headaches.

Walter and Eliza began an intense series of love-letters, which her sister Emilie published in 1933. Walter missed Eliza badly, and was scathing about "the rubbing doctor", convinced he was a charlatan who aimed to keep her in Edinburgh as long as possible. In a letter from Herd's Hill on 22 November he wrote: "What is the particular advantage of being rubbed at *Edinburgh*? Since yesterday I have made careful enquiries and am assured that the English can rub. Why not be rubbed in Somersetshire? Let the doctor mark the place and have a patch put to show where to let an able-bodied party in the West of England rub on the same place and surely it will be as well?"

He determined to visit her in the Scottish capital and arrived there on Sunday 13 December. On Wednesday 15 December (Eliza's 25th birthday), the couple exchanged engagement rings and, for her birthday, Walter gave her several small volumes of poetry by Wordsworth, Keats and Shelley, bound in red calf.

His views on marriage seemed to have moved on during the previous 6 years. In a letter of 26 June 1851 to his friend, Richard Holt Hutton, congratulating him on his forthcoming marriage, he had commented, "I should have thought myself that it is a great deal of trouble being married & that it would require rather to be borne under condolence - but as you seem to be pleased at it, I am pleased also." Hutton, in his later *Memoir* of Bagehot, recalled that he "used to say banteringly to his mother, by way of putting her off at a time when she was anxious for him to marry, 'A man's mother is his misfortune, but his wife is his fault.'"

Wedding, honeymoon and new home

Walter and Eliza's wedding took place on Wednesday 21 April 1858 at Claverton, which the Wilsons had rented since 1855. The bridal party left the Manor at around 11am, and the marriage ceremony at the local church was performed by Rev William Hale, Rector of Claverton. Eliza wore a dress of white velvet, with Honiton lace veil, and a wreath of roses and orange flowers.

Neither of Walter's parents attended – his mother was not well enough for such an event, and his father stayed behind to be with her. However, a Bagehot cousin, Mary Watson Bagehot, was a flower girl, and a Stuckey cousin, Vincent Wood, was Walter's best man. Vincent Wood later changed his surname to Stuckey in accordance with his grandmother Julia's will, and so, when he later became head of Stuckey's Bank, he was the second 'Vincent Stuckey' to do so.

Eliza's diary entry summed up the day rather crisply:

> Our wedding day. Beautiful and hot. Church quite full. Used our pew for vestry. Walked on lawn after church. Hanoverian band played. At breakfast Mr Moffatt proposed our health. Sir William Topham proposed the bridesmaids in a very clever speech. Over at 2:30. Walter and I started in post chariot at 3:30. Numbers of Bath people had arrived for the dance. I went into morning room to see them. Six white satin slippers thrown after us. We drove to Frome, changed horses, and took up luggage, and got to Stourton at 7.

A letter from Walter to his mother two days into the honeymoon provided more details. He had already sent her a brief note in pencil from their Frome stop, which simply informed her that "*We* are married. Everything went off well, and my wife sends her love." Dated 23 April, from Stourton on the Somerset/Wiltshire border, he wrote:

> I am scarcely an impartial judge, but it seemed to me a very bright affair and that not only the persons married but the others enjoyed themselves, which generally they do not. Nobody shed a single tear. Eliza was a most composed bride – a little anxious at the crisis, but very cheerful after it was over. Vincent Wood made a splendid 'best man' only that the multitude *would* think he was the bridegroom. Mary was much admired and all the bridesmaids were very animated and nice. There was wonderful oration at the Breakfast. A Mr Moffatt (MP for Ashburton) proposed *our* health in a copious and eloquent manner, and spoke of the 'hundreds of thousands' who had read my writings, whom I myself should wish to see particularly. Sir William Topham proposed the health of the bridesmaids in a very clever speech in a sort of Lord Palmerston style. He is a man about the Court, Captain of the Yeomen of the Guard and understands the 'touch and go' style of oratory rather well. My attention was rather, however, distracted from what he said by wondering that '*that* man' should be speaking at my wedding. Few people seem so far off my beat. I believe that the dance too after we went away was also successful, and the day was so gorgeous that I think it made people cheerful. Mind *will* tell especially in the weather. We had a delicious drive to this place and have done nothing but potter about it ever since. Eliza is a trifle tired by the crisis, but very well and seems able to endure futurity. The post is going so I must leave off. With best love to my father.

In a touching addition at the end of the letter, Eliza added a postscript: "I am your affectionate daughter, Eliza Bagehot. This is the *first* time I have signed my *new* name."

Press reports gave a little more detail of the festivities, especially after the happy couple left at 3:30. What was described as a "continuous stream of company" of at least 200 guests from London and the local community began arriving from 3pm, being received by the bride's parents for a *fête champêtre*, i.e. a garden party. Dancing began at 3, and continued until 9pm, in good weather, on the lawn and in the ballroom. Many of the company wandered around Claverton's extensive grounds or were "enjoying the hospitality of the kind host and hostess."

After a brief stay at Stourton, Walter and Eliza spent the rest of their honeymoon touring Devon by coach and by train, visiting places such as Dawlish, Plymouth, Bideford, Ilfracombe and Teignmouth. Walter wrote several brief notes to his father, and the couple read a great deal of Matthew Arnold's poetry, theologian Frederick Denison Maurice's sermons and John Henry Newman's *Lyra Apostolica* (a collection of sacred poems). At the end of May they travelled through West Somerset, catching a train at Bridgwater for Clevedon. There they settled in to their new home on the hills around the town, *The Arches* (renamed by them from its original *Bella Vista*) which they had rented from Sir Arthur Elton of Clevedon Court.

Clevedon was regarded as a convenient location for Walter in particular. As he had advised his friend Hutton that January, "If you live in the country, live near the shores of a railway – quite near, it is a great saving of mind and anxiety. I wish I may be able to. I must live 'somewhere' between Bristol and Langport."

In recognition of the changes in his circumstances, both personal and professional, over recent months, Walter wished to live nearer to Bristol. He explained this in a letter to Eliza of 7 December 1857: 'Entre nous however one of my reasons for wishing to be away next week is that I am making some propositions to my partners in the Bank which wd. facilitate my living near Bristol and it is only proper that I shd. not be present when they are discussed."

The Bank duly obliged and decided that same month that he "should attend the Bristol Bank 3 or 4 days a week and share in its management and responsibilities and spend the rest of his time at Langport and elsewhere in discharge of his other duties" at a revised salary of £500 a year. His responsibilities at the Bank, especially the important Bristol operation, continued to grow. In June the following year, for instance, he was authorised to sign cash-notes and other such documents as one of the Bristol Bank department managers (at the same time, James Wilson was allowed, after some discussion, to buy 100 Bank shares). Clevedon would allow easier travel to Bristol, as well as to Langport, and for visits by the young couple to her family at Claverton.

A week after their arrival at Clevedon the protracted wedding events concluded with the couple meeting their respective new families and friends, beginning with a trip to Herd's Hill for *sitting up*, a West Country tradition where a new bride received guests, followed by a family gathering at The Arches, then a stay in London before finally returning to Clevedon.

Multitasking

The newlyweds' life settled down into its new rhythm, with Walter spending much of his time commuting between Clevedon, Langport, London and Bristol, and much social activity with their respective families and friends (especially the Huttons) in the first three of these places. In London, the Wilsons' social and political connections were introducing Walter to a more elevated stratum of metropolitan society, and his confidence grew about the scope and intensity of his writing ambitions.

Not all his literary ventures were successful. His collection of early profiles, burdened with the plodding title, *Estimates of Some Englishmen and Scotchmen*, had been published in January 1858 to a mixture of negative reviews, where it was even reviewed at all. Walter defended its publication in a letter of 4 January to his then fiancée, as having been intended for her to read, "because they will help you to understand my mind better than anything else. You may consider the book in the nature of a 'love letter'. It never would have been put together but from a floating idea that perhaps you might read it and perhaps you might like me better for it. We shall see." That he then went on to ponder the nature of reputation and posterity suggests that he knew what its reception beyond Eliza would be.

He was far more successful with a *National Review* article of January 1859 on parliamentary reform, a major political issue at the time. Its reception was such that it was speedily turned into a pamphlet in March. Though his proposals were rather modest - Walter was never a true democrat, certainly not one in favour of rule by what he regarded as the ignorant masses - it shone a fresh ray of light into what was a long-running and stalemated issue at the heart of British government and politics, which divided the country, the classes, and within and across the main parties.

James Wilson was keen for Walter to capitalise on this opportunity, and threw a dinner party at his London home in his honour on April 1 with a guest list that Bagehot himself described as "a very fine collection of public animals." They included a number of very senior politicians, including William Gladstone himself, and this triggered what would be a long and mutually fruitful professional collaboration and friendship with Gladstone throughout the rest of Bagehot's life.

At the same time, he had to attend to his family business duties, especially at the Bank, entailing spending time mainly in Bristol and London, and attending Directors' meetings there and elsewhere, since he had been made their Secretary in 1856. In July 1859, as an example noted in Eliza' diary, he even had to spend some time dealing with a case of a dishonest clerk in Bristol.

Responsibilities at *The Economist*

Amid all this busy life, another series of events occurred which changed the trajectory of his life. These concerned his employer, father-in-law and mentor, James Wilson, whose ministerial career was becoming a burden. He had even been vetoed as the proposed Governor of the Victoria colony in Australia in 1856 by the Queen herself as not being "at all proper person" for such an important post, which should go to "a man of higher position and standing and who could represent his Sovereign adequately." When, in the summer of 1859, he was offered the chance of becoming in effect India's Chancellor of the Exchequer in Calcutta, he decided after much thought to accept this intriguing new challenge, as he had had an interest both in finance and in Indian affairs.

Besides all the upheaval this move would cause to himself and his family, the question of the running of *The Economist* was clearly something to be addressed. Bagehot by then was clearly Wilson's right-hand man, more than a mere employee and son-in-law, and what emerged was what Wilson described in a letter to a ministerial colleague as "my friend Bagehot has undertaken a sort of general superintendence of *The Economist* and Hutton remains editor under him." The pecking order in the Wilson empire was now clear, and Bagehot was at its heart. There was a protracted handover, as Wilson meticulously prepared himself for his new role, before he sailed for India in late October. This involved, amongst other matters, Bagehot helping him write his will into the late hours on 13 October, "a cheerful topic", as Walter wryly wrote to Eliza the following day.

While Walter doubtless appreciated the trust so vested in him, the scale and weight of these new responsibilities were enormous, especially in addition to his family banking career, and his other commitments like the running of the *National Review*. For all his recent successes, and the many contacts Wilson made for him, he was still more of an outside observer in London society and politics. He feared that he was out of his depth without Wilson's presence.

That his close friend, Hutton, had turned not to be an effective editor added to his burden, as did the appearance in 1860 of a new competitor, *The Money Market Review* (much later transformed into the successful *Investors Chronicle*), though Wilson, by letter from India, sought to reassure him about the impact of the latter.

The Bank were willing to assist him in coping with these new burdens by agreeing, in mid-December 1859, to Walter's written request to alter his banking responsibilities, especially in relation to duties at Langport, though it would not affect his Bristol duties. It was noted by the Bank that this opportunity to do more of benefit to the Bank, while having to be in London - which Walter had estimated at being 2-3 days every fortnight - would be "very desirable."

Amid all the pressure, Walter could console himself that it would end at some point, when Wilson returned from India, and something like the previous state of affairs would return, with the added bonus of having had some years of invaluable experience and opportunity.

Walter and Eliza, along with various other members of the Wilson family and entourage, managed to fit in a brief vacation in Paris. Walter found it stimulating, though a later letter from W R Greg to another Wilson sister did not paint a very rosy picture of the trio, with widespread illness among the party, and his disgust at the antics of the Bagehots: "You never saw such people as Walter and Eliza for appetite and unpunctuality."

The couple then added a further few days in Germany, to consult a noted eye specialist for their persistent headaches and eye troubles, before returning home. It was during that latter trip that Bagehot was approached by Hutton to stand for Parliament as a Liberal for London University, the first of many of Walter's flirtations with parliamentary elections.

More unexpected developments

As 1860 progressed, with Walter extremely busy at his various responsibilities, yet another unexpected event intervened to alter the course of his life. Wilson had been having a very difficult time in India, trying to carry out his financial policies in the face of opposition there and at home. In August he contracted dysentery and died on the 11th in Calcutta. However it took four weeks for the devastating news to reach home, and the family first learned of Wilson's death via a newspaper report in mid-September, while the Bagehots were at Clevedon, a day before they received official word from the Government.

James Wilson's tomb in Kolkata, India

Under the terms of Wilson's will, Bagehot was an executor, alongside three of James Wilson's brothers, and he assumed control of the situation as the de facto new head of the Wilson family and their affairs. In a letter of 24 September to his brother-in-law William Halsey (who had married Sophie Wilson in 1859) he wrote of his personal reaction to the news: "It was in the strictest sense awful news - at least to me. ... Especially in Mr. Wilson's case. I never really contemplated the contingency of his death ... I have never felt the shock of any event so much." He wrote a heartfelt memoir of his father-in-law, which was published as a special supplement to the 17 November issue of *The Economist*. The Government offered the vacant post to Bagehot, but he refused it, because of his Langport family commitments.

The other executors made Bagehot permanent director of *The Economist*, thereby formalising what was intended to be a temporary arrangement during Wilson's absence. To clear more space for his enhanced responsibilities in London he resigned as Manager of the Bristol branch of the Bank, though he remained its Secretary and assumed formal supervision of the Bank's London activities. On a personal level, the Bagehots realised they would now need to be based in London, and so gave up their Clevedon home in early 1861, and stayed in a series of temporary lodgings, before moving in with the Wilson family at their home at 12 Upper Belgrave Street sometime around the turn of the year.

The final act in this momentous transition was the departure of Hutton as editor of *The Economist* in 1861, when he moved to help revive *The Spectator*. This neatly solved Bagehot's problems with his friend's unhappy tenure, and enabled Walter to become formally editor of *The Economist*, a role he held until his death.

CHAPTER EIGHT

Running The Economist

The dramatic events of 1857-60 which catapulted Bagehot from being a 'literary banker' to editor of *The Economist* set in train the last 17 years of his life. Instead of being a country banker who also wrote essays for serious journals, he was now running a major, influential news magazine, being editor, manager and chief writer all rolled into one.

Such a role may have come to him in the fullness of time, even without the appearance of the Wilsons, perhaps through a gradual gravitation to London and a growing literary reputation, but not so suddenly to a young man in his early thirties with – his then relatively limited Bank jobs and his involvement in the *National Review* apart – little or no relevant experience. He was no longer just writing for pleasure; he now had additional onerous professional and legal responsibilities, not only to his small staff at *The Economist*, but also to the Wilsons. They were not just (relatively newly related) family, but as beneficiaries of James Wilson's estate - of which Bagehot was a co-trustee - his ultimate boss, as proprietors of *The Economist*.

It was a daunting challenge, which must have, at times, seemed to overwhelm him. To what extent his constant ill-health was an effect of that pressure or a cause, is an open question. That he was so successful in his vastly expanded role is a testament to his inner strength as well as his abilities.

Ruth Dudley Edwards' magisterial 1993 history of *The Economist*, *The pursuit of reason*, contains a comprehensive account of Bagehot, both as contributor and editor, which should be read by anyone wishing to have 'the whole story' of this aspect of his life. This chapter seeks simply to provide an overview of his role as editor/manager, that vital part of Bagehot's later years, which, though not the main foundation of his enduring reputation, formed a significant part of it.

Editing *The Economist*

As editor, he was responsible for the content of *The Economist*, soliciting articles and weighing up unsolicited contributions or proposals, and his letters of the period provide a flavour of him doing such tasks. For example, he wrote (from home) to Professor John Cairnes, a noted economist, on 30 May 1863 thanking him for a contribution (on the value of gold) which had just been published, and assuring him that "I shall be most happy to insert in the Economist any more which you may write on that subject."

In a pair of letters in late 1869, he deftly dealt with Edward Robert Bulwer Lytton (son of the noted novelist and politician). In the first, he apologised for not writing sooner – because he thought his contributions "would be more likely to be properly appreciated when the annual holiday is over and politicians were returned to their mill" – and offered to leave the choice of subjects to him "as the public generally like best to read that which the author likes most to write." In a follow up message, after Lytton's first (and only) piece had been published, Bagehot flatteringly wrote "if you have leisure to send me now and then a few of such letters on points which come before you, and which you know I think the English public will value them ... The subjects which strike you as interesting will probably be those too on which the correspondence will be most interesting."

One aspect of this was to include views and opinions in *The Economist* that Bagehot, as editor, did not want to be regarded as the paper's, or his own, policy, so he would ask others to contribute signed pieces. For example, he wrote to his friend (and future co-editor after Bagehot's death), Robert Palgrave on 24 March 1875: "I shall be most happy to print anything from you in the Ecst. to show that the strain on the Bank of England would be augmented by the abolition of the country circulation, and I would rather you shd put your name to it as I am very anxious to keep the Economist from even seeming to be an advocate of the subject."

Bagehot's ever-growing insider status in gathering news and information would help create *The Economist*'s insightful content. Especially after he became editor, Bagehot seems to have had access to state papers, including those which would certainly be thought of as confidential today. For instance in 1865 he wrote to Earl Grey to "return to you the Cabinet Minutes which you were so very kind as to lend me." The papers he referred to related to the Earl's father who had been the Whig Prime Minister at the time of the Great Reform Act.

There were also occasions where Ministers gave *The Economist* a confidential 'steer'. In late 1862, Charles Villiers, a Cabinet minister, was anxious about the Lancashire economy due to the American Civil War's impact on cotton imports. He wrote to Bagehot: "I do not know if any notice will be taken in the Economist of Lancashire distress this week, but, in case there should be, I merely send this document, which was prepared for the Cabinet only, that any figures might be corrected by it if that was thought worth while. ... Perhaps you will have the goodness to let me have it back after examining it, which, as it is quite correct, you might wish to do."

A similar type of high-level request occurred in October 1870 regarding the Franco-Prussian war, when the Foreign Secretary, Earl Granville, wrote a confidential letter to him, using diplomatic but clear language:

> May I ask you in anything you say, which always comes with so much weight both from the high character of your paper and the great ability of the articles, not to write anything which will give thoughtful Germans reason to believe that they have just cause of complaint against US. You will believe me when I say the request is exclusively on public grounds.

No doubt Bagehot would have received similar entreaties over his years at the helm of *The Economist* by other more private means, whether in the numerous direct professional or social meetings he had with senior politicians and officials, or through intermediaries.

Staffing *The Economist*

Through its early years, including those when Bagehot was connected with it, *The Economist* was run by a very small core staff at 340 The Strand. He described himself in 1873 as "Manager, Editor and principal-writer on business subjects", often writing as many as three or four of the leading articles himself. As was common in those days, virtually all articles, except for those by guest authors or letter-writers, were unsigned. For much of his time as editor he was assisted by what was usually described as a part-time statistician (William Newmarch) and "a few clerks".

Bagehot's office was on the first-floor front room overlooking The Strand, described by the housekeeper as 'a well-furnished apartment, with a nice sofa.' Apparently, even after his death in 1877, the staff retained fond memories of him in these old offices, as a later recruit, Albert Chapman, who joined in 1898 as an office-boy, recounted in a 1942 memoir: "it seemed to me as though Mr Bagehot was still living in the memory of the people who were working on The Economist.... Mr Bagehot ... used to keep his coachman waiting outside seeming to forget the passage of time so deeply was he absorbed in his work."

The Economist offices in the Strand, London

In 1868, due to his ill-health, he recruited Robert Giffen as 'assistant editor', writing many of the business pieces – often being the editor's mouthpiece in relaying his views to readers - and generally supporting Bagehot's heavy load. When illness necessitated it, Giffen would visit Bagehot at his home in London, to discuss these tasks. One of the last letters we have during Bagehot's lifetime provides both a flavour of this enduring collaboration between the two men, even after Giffen had formally left the paper in 1876, and also the unexpectedness of Bagehot's sudden demise.

Giffen wrote from his post at the Board of Trade to Bagehot on Thursday 22 March 1877, expressing concern at the contents of a telegram he had received from him – "I hope you have not been overdoing your work lately, as it is so easy to do." - and making himself available, having got various papers for a proposed article on bankruptcy (which duly appeared in the paper). After a few other bits of business, he signed off, unaware of how gravely ill Bagehot was.

Developing *The Economist*

Bagehot knew that *The Economist* needed to develop and change over time, rather than rest on its Wilsonian laurels. Just as Wilson had added business-related supplements – such as *The Railway Monitor* in 1845 to address the railway investment bubble - Bagehot introduced additions including the annual *Commercial History*, the *Investors' Monthly Manual* and a *Banking Supplement*. He expanded coverage of international political and economic news through a web of foreign correspondents.

He homed in on *The Economist*'s core mission as a business and financial publication, as he set out in an 1873 memorandum to the Wilson family on the paper. "Every other part of the Economist must now be considered second to that which concerns the money market, as far as the profitableness of the paper is concerned." Noting that the original focus of Wilson's paper on Free Trade was a battle which had been won, "[t]he natural changes in trade are all which can now be discussed - and of these the changes in the money market are the most important because they affect all men of business, and all are anxious to see what will be their course."

To that end, he believed that political coverage and the like shouldn't be included just for its own sake but:

> must be viewed mainly with reference to the tastes of men of business. It is among them and among them only that the Economist will ever circulate, and political articles would injure the paper, if they excluded necessary business matter or if they were not such as men of business would care to read. But if properly written they are a material support to the paper and strengthen its circulation: indeed if politics were abandoned there wd. be a universal impression that the paper had changed its character and was going down.

One biographer, Alastair Buchan, described *The Economist* under Bagehot when dealing with political or social issues of the day as "a sort of one man Royal Commission especially upon social problems, asking questions as much as attempting an answer. In the process he quietly softened much of the hard middle class dogmatism that he had inherited."

An especially significant focus was the concentration on sophisticated statistics to enhance the articles. The use of statistics was an important aspect of *The Economist's* approach from its inception under Wilson. Bagehot continued that approach, though unlike Wilson his aversion to detail hardly made him a natural statistician.

His assistant editor, Robert Giffen, himself a noted statistician, recognised this dichotomy when he wrote of Bagehot having "a 'quantitative' sense - his knowledge and feeling of the 'how much' in dealing with the complex working of economic tendencies" despite "a repugnance to minute detail, including an aversion to manipulate figures, all but amounting to inability to 'add up'." He explained:

The petty detail which most people find easy enough was beyond measure irksome to him; and the irksomeness was aggravated, when I knew him, by weak eyesight. But columns of figures are not statistics, though they are the raw material of statisticians; and this Bagehot fully proved by his remarkable appreciation of the numerical element in economic problems, all the while he had these technical difficulties in his way. In this quality he was second to no statistician I have ever met, and infinitely superior to most. ... irksome as the detail of figures was to him, and naturally also the detail of constructing statistical tables, he was a singularly good judge and critic of such tables and the results they brought out. He knew what tables could be made to say, and the value of simplicity in their construction. He had an intense dislike of that vice of almost all amateur statisticians, and not a few experts, the attempt to put too much into their tables. He likewise laid down a rule which I have found invaluable for the preparation of all accounts and statistical tables: that after you have had the most accurate clerks to do them, you should not 'pass' them without having them examined by an expert in the subject, who would be able, if there was occasion, to detect something substantially and flagrantly wrong which had escaped the notice of the mechanical compilers. Thus he was not a statistician in the technical sense, perhaps, and so could not be the authority on some subjects he was sometimes supposed to be; but he possessed the essential qualifications for dealing with and reflecting on statistical data when they came in his way, and a sufficient sense of quantity to lean upon and to guide him in his own studies and writing.

Robert Giffen, Assistant Editor

As well as Giffen on the statistical front, Bagehot also employed from 1863 William Newmarch, whom he had long admired. Newmarch's initial job was the creation of the annual *Commercial History*, which was designed to be a comprehensive and indispensable reference book for the paper's readers. He also produced many specialised pieces for the paper, and refined and improved its statistics so as to provide readers with useful information from the data, such as changes over time, rather than just annual lists of raw data. These techniques were gradually adopted both in the private sector and in government to study phenomena like trade cycles (a subject in which Bagehot had a great interest).

Statistics are only as good as those selecting, compiling or interpreting them, and such a novel approach at that time would risk errors in their application. A recent analysis of *The Economist's* leading articles during the mid-1860s concluded that the use of 'bad' statistics led Bagehot and his paper astray as to the nature, impact and duration of economic 'bubbles', with too much focus being made on the banking panics caused by the collapse of the noted house of Overend Gurney in 1866, and too little on similar problems elsewhere, such as the railway industry.

Bagehot recognised that the theory of the science of political economy was not the same as the 'real' world of trade and commerce occupied by his core readership, 'men of business', and while statistics – carefully constructed and properly applied – could help in some measure to bridge that gap, they were not a complete answer. Figures in a table may be seen as facts on the one hand, but on the other, as things that can be manipulated. So with prices, "at the outset there is a difference between the men of theory and the men of practice. Theorists take a table of prices as facts settled by unalterable laws; a stockbroker will tell you such prices can be 'made'. In actual business such is his constant expression." Bagehot could usually see the practical realities of life, especially commercial life beyond the theories and scientific methods.

Managing *The Economist*

As manager/director of *The Economist*, and a co-trustee of James Wilson's estate, Bagehot had executive responsibilities to discharge. These are conveniently viewed through his 19 July 1873 Memorandum to the Wilson family about the state of the estate's finances, especially relating to *The Economist*. The paper formed a large part of these assets and income, which he warned them "must never be depended upon like any ordinary investment."

While the past year (1872) had been the paper's most profitable ever, it had followed a long period since 1866 when it wasn't so successful, due, he advised, both to competition from other publications and by the post-panic era of calm resulting in there being "nothing to tell the public about it." The recent upswing had resulted from a more 'interesting' money market, which *The Economist* was best placed to exploit, due, he modestly attributed, to his own "rather peculiar position" as a senior banker in Stuckey's Bank, which had large sums placed in London, thereby providing him with "better means of knowing than a mere writer what is happening and what is likely to happen."

He considered his own position in the running of the paper, and, presciently as it turned out less than four years later, how it would have to be filled "if anything happened to me." A successor, he advised, would need to have a share in the paper (something, Bagehot, as a trustee, could not legally hold), and "[n]o reliance must ever be placed on a mere salaried manager or Editor." In the course of this advice, we learn about Bagehot's remuneration, doubtless taking into account this inability to share in its ownership.

> But as the best substitute it was arranged between my cotrustees and myself that I should have a salary of £400 a year as Editor and Manager, be paid for my writing at the customary rate of the paper, and have half the profits above £2,000 a year whenever the paper yielded more than £2,000. The income of the property of the paper was a little less than £2,000 when Mr Wilson went to India and when the paper came into my hands. My

remuneration from these sources has been very variable as for several years the paper did not yield as much as £2,000, and sometimes it yielded very considerably more. On the average it has been £780 a year since 1862. I should say that of late I have paid part of the cost of a sub Editor out of my £400 as I have not since my illness been able to do all which I used to do formerly.

He then discussed the actual management of the paper, claiming that "there is an increase of difficulty in managing the paper because the detail of the business subjects of which it treats continually grows", a trend which he addressed way of new supplements and off-shoots. A key ingredient of the paper was that it had no potentially conflicting interests above it (what he called "a shop behind it"), ensuring its valued independence, and which would be threatened by a more 'conventional' and less 'family-connected' salaried editor.

Even with a small staff, and what would be regarded as a small circulation of around 3,000 – albeit an influential elite readership domestically and abroad – running *The Economist* was no mean challenge, especially for someone who had so many other activities and responsibilities, and was not in the best of health. That his tenure has widely been recognised as one of, if not the, greatest in the paper's 180-year history is an important pillar of his enduring reputation and legacy. Ruth Dudley Edwards expressed this best in her 1993 history of *The Economist*:

> He took James Wilson's creation, broadened it, deepened it, enriched it and made of it a product with a life of its own. Bagehot got the formula right, won for the paper a solid reputation and made it so sturdy that it could live without him.

The three eldest Wilson sisters: Eliza, b.1832, Julia, b.1834 and Matilda, b.1836.
Proprietors, with other family members, of The Economist

CHAPTER NINE
Political ambitions

Walter Bagehot had, for some years, made efforts to become a Member of Parliament. All of them were unsuccessful. Why that was the case was probably easier to answer than the question of why he would even try at all. Did he really want to be an MP?

He had made himself over time a master of the theory and, in particular, the practice of politics and government, and this might have led him to assume that he was uniquely equipped to enter the House of Commons. Perhaps he was gravely mistaken. As one much later critic put it, "Practice proved to be less exhilarating than theory."

Despite the gradual extension of the franchise and reforms of electoral practice, standing for election was still a very different experience from the public scrutiny and exposure of modern times. Those faults which emerged during his attempts, such as being a poor public speaker, need not necessarily have been fatal. That his 'set' of political views, such as they were, did not fit neatly into any one political party's creed - that he could be described as either or both a conservative Liberal or a liberal Conservative - was not that problematic in the political party flux that prevailed in mid-19th century Britain.

He fully appreciated the prestige of being an MP, as he wrote in an 1874 essay:

> [A] man gains far more social standing, as it is called, by going into Parliament than he can gain in any other way. ... As long as English society considers a seat in Parliament a great social prize, a seat there will, by the mass of Englishmen, be looked for and coveted as such. And it is very natural that it should be so regarded as such a prize - it is far more comprehensible to most people than eminence in science or literature. ... To take part in the government of the country - to be a member of the assembly which rules the country - is a distinction much more intelligible to most people than to have written a book or made a discovery in optics; and it is also a more indisputable distinction. ... It is an indisputable mark of comprehensible merit ...

On the other hand, his sister-in-law and biographer, Emilie Barrington believed that though he genuinely made serious efforts to become an MP himself, "he had no fervent faith in the advantages of a Parliamentary career, no belief that it could aid the higher life - at all events not his higher life." She believed that he did so largely to please his mother – an understandable feeling, especially given her state of mind - who was very ambitious for her beloved son. His growing successes over the years were not enough for her: "His position was not sufficiently defined to please her. That distinguished politicians held a high opinion of him was not enough, she wished him to be a distinguished politician himself."

He readily recognised his own failings as a practical politician, that he was, as he put it himself, "between sizes in politics." Yet a part of him hankered after such a position. In late December 1861 he told his wife, Eliza, that, despite the Bridgwater constituency's notorious reputation for electoral corruption, he wished to become its MP. And he never seemed to have lost this ambition. Giving a paper to the Metaphysical Society, at the Grosvenor Hotel, London on 13 December 1870, he confessed:

Some years ago I stood for a borough in the West of England, and after a keen contest was defeated by seven. Almost directly afterwards there was accidentally another election, and, as I would not stand, another candidate of my own side was elected, and I of course ceased to have any hold upon the place, or chance of being elected there. But for years I had the deepest conviction that I should be "Member for Bridgwater"; and no amount of reasoning would get it out of my head. The borough is now disfranchised; but even still, if I allow my mind to dwell on the contest, – if I think of the hours I was ahead in the morning, and the rush of votes at two o'clock by which I was defeated, – and even more, if I call up the image of the nomination day, with all the people's hands outstretched, and all their excited faces looking the more different on account of their identity in posture, the old feeling almost comes back upon me, and for a moment I believe that I shall be Member for Bridgwater.

Early opportunities

There were some possibilities, and there were occasional press reports of him in connection with various seats, such as Bristol in December 1866. Another was about him being adopted in 1860 as the Liberal candidate for the proposed new London University seat, but nothing came of it, and the seat was not even created until the 1867 Reform Act. He first heard of the proposal in a letter from Hutton he received at Cologne on his way home from his continental trip to France and Germany in early 1860. Hutton and Bagehot's friend, Timothy Smith Osler, were on a committee of graduates looking for potential candidates, and were keen on Bagehot. Walter thought it over during his journey back to Britain, but decided against it.

However, when he got back to Herd's Hill, he found that his parents were strongly in favour of the proposal, so he contacted Smith Osler asking that the possibility be kept open, at least until he was back in London. At a meeting of the University's graduates, he himself proposed Sir John Romilly, who had been an MP until defeated in 1852, and was currently a judge (Master of the Rolls). Despite this, Bagehot himself secured the meeting's support. On 2 April, a worried Eliza wrote to her father, concerned about "what Papa Bagehot will say for he is so very prudent, and has such a dread of Walter being a poor member of Parliament." She was clearly concerned about their finances at that time, as in her diary, she estimated Walter's income at £1000 a year, but their outgoings were £1400 a year.

There was much internal politicking among the supporters of the various 'candidates', but, as Walter wrote to Eliza that month, "The tide is setting in favour of Romilly as I always said it would." Romilly finally emerged as the favoured nominee, but the matter was rendered moot for the time being when the proposed Reform Bill did not make it into law. London University was not enfranchised until the 1867 Reform Act, when Bagehot was again in the running.

After he refused an invitation in early May 1865 to stand for Dudley, he did try at Manchester that year. On 10 June, after seeing Gladstone, he wrote him a solicitous letter asking if he could give him a letter of support – what he characteristically termed an 'intellectual certificate' – as he knew (or claimed to know) that he, Bagehot, was a public figure:

> As I mentioned to you the Liberal party in Manchester are in search of a candidate and I have been told that 'if could get well introduced' I might have some chance. The only title

which I can have to such an honor is that I have devoted much time and labour to the Commercial and economical subjects in which Manchester is so much interested. But my writings on such subjects having been published anonymously my name is not well known to the public in connection with them. It would therefore be of the very greatest value to me if you could give me any sort of 'intellectual certificate' especially if you thought you could conscientiously say I could be at all useful in the House of Commons on such subjects.

Gladstone duly obliged two days later, although it was hardly a ringing endorsement, focussing entirely on Bagehot's qualifications for Parliament: "If thorough acquaintance with economical science, extensive and accurate knowledge, ready and practical habits of business, and a conciliatory disposition, go to fit a man for the representation of these great national interests, it certainly appears to me that your fitness must stand without dispute in the first rank."

William Ewart Gladstone when he was Chancellor of the Exchequer

As the electioneering in Manchester progressed, Bagehot remained reasonably hopeful, but knew that his fate would likely be decided at a large public meeting held on 3 July, which, in addition to their Conservative opponents being there, meant he would have to face a large, potentially hostile audience who did not know who this Southerner was. This unknown carpetbagger label was neatly expressed by a heckler who asked why a London constituency, where he would be better known, hadn't nominated him already. From the press reports, it was clear that it was a very difficult meeting for Bagehot, where his poor public oratory was exposed, and his chances destroyed. Eliza summed it up in her diary:" 'Walter spoke at a meeting in the Town Hall at Manchester, to about 400 people, but was badly received and gave up standing:"

Walter himself accepted his failure, as he later wrote to his parents: "I tried to get into Parliament for Manchester this year, but Manchester could not 'see it', I had a letter from Mr. Gladstone recommending me, but it was of no use. They said, "If he is so celebrated, why does not Finsbury elect him?" Publicly, he explained himself in a letter to a newspaper in August, which was widely reported. While acknowledging that "the events of an unsuccessful candidature do not, I fear, interest the public", he tried to explain his reason for standing, amidst the discord in the city amongst the various Liberal factions, from the moderates to the Radicals, "It was not my object to divide the Liberal party but to combine it."

Bridgwater and its aftermath

His chance to stand in his 'dream seat' of Bridgwater eventually came in a by-election caused by the unseating of one of its two MPs, the Tory, Henry Westropp, in April 1866. Westropp had topped the two-member poll at the general election the previous year, but a House of Commons Committee found him guilty of corrupt practices, and voided his election.

The first hint is in Eliza's diary entry of 3 May 1866: "Walter saw Mr Brand [presumably Sir Henry Brand, Liberal chief whip and future Speaker of the House of Commons] & settled to be the liberal candidate at forthcoming election for Bridgwater." In 1869, Walter said the first approach was by three senior Liberals visiting him at his London home very soon after Westropp had been unseated. Because of Bridgwater's electoral notoriety, he had already consulted his solicitor, George Robins, about the matter. One scholar of Bridgwater's electoral history of that period commented that "given Bagehot's background, it is a mystery" that he was not approached for the 1865 general election as Bagehot was "an ideal candidate for Bridgwater."

Over the following weeks, Eliza's diary records Walter's progress towards standing, including receiving two deputations from Bridgwater on 12 and 14 May. At the latter meeting, he "gave his answer, promising to come forward as the liberal candidate for B'water, whenever the writ is issued, but not before."

On Sunday 27 May, Bridgwater's Liberal MP, Alexander Kinglake called "to tell Walter he believed the writ for Bridgwater will be issued this week." The writ for the by-election was duly issued in the Commons on Thursday 31 May, after an unsuccessful attempt by some MPs to have a select committee set up to examine alleged corrupt practices at Bridgwater elections. Walter went down to the House to check that it was being issued, and the following day, Friday 1 June, he went to Bridgwater to begin his campaign.

He left London at 2pm by train and arrived at 7, where, as he later described it, he "was received here, of course, in the usual tumultuous manner according to the habit of this place." According to Eliza's diary, "he was met by 4000 people, farmers & 4 grey horses etc, & addressed the people from the carriage on the Cornhill." His speech was brief optimistically predicting that the large, welcoming crowd "augers well [and] betokens a coming triumph." He urged his supporters to "fight the contest honestly and well", echoing his previous insistence to his main backers on a 'pure' campaign, and assured the crowd that he was "a true and sincere Liberal."

The next day, he called on the prominent Liberals of the borough, and made his first major speech that evening, to a party meeting at the Assembly Rooms, George Street. He confirmed his support for the current Liberal Government, headed by the Prime Minister, Earl Russell, and the Chancellor, William Gladstone, and stressed his, and his family's, commercial connections with Bridgwater, contrasting them with the Scottish background of his Tory opponent, George Patton.

He played the 'English card', criticising Patton as a Scots lawyer: "I wonder very much that the party which possesses such zeal for old English institutions cannot find an English representative ... Being represented by a Scotchman is being represented by a man unknown. He knows nothing of you, and you can find out very little about him ...

Scotland, you will feel, is not the same sort of place as Bridgwater. There is a perfectly different system of laws there. He can't help you with English laws ..."

On Sunday 3 June, he went to church with the Corporation of Bridgwater in the morning, before paying a quick visit to Langport for two hours in the afternoon. Monday was spent canvassing in Bridgwater all day, as was Tuesday, followed by a party meeting in the evening at the Assembly Rooms.

Wednesday 6 June was the great day of the nomination hustings in front of the Market House. Walter responded to criticism of his attacks on Patton as a Scot, denying that he was anti-Scottish, merely claiming that local candidates were better than those from afar. The main thrust of his brief address was the ongoing parliamentary battles over the latest Reform Bill to extend the franchise: "we are for a living Constitution; but our opponents would hand down to their descendants a mummy Constitution."

Bridgwater election: Bagehot speaking to a crowd at the Cornhill

The event was a rowdy and at times violent occasion, and, though the Liberals were confident of victory, a show of hands fell in Patton's favour. Eliza dryly remarked in her diary: "The Mayor a Tory." All depended now on the poll itself the following day, Thursday 7 June.

Walter had a clear early lead among the very small electorate, but this faded as the day wore on, as recorded by Eliza: "8.15am: Bagehot 29, Patton 14, 10.15am: Bagehot 230, Patton 197, Tie at 1.15 291, 4pm: Patton 301, Bagehot 294." So, he had lost by 7 votes. A crestfallen Bagehot briefly addressed the crowd, conceding defeat and hoping t would not be long before the Liberals could retake the seat. He then returned to his family home at Herd's Hill, outside Langport, and went back the following morning to Bridgwater, spending the day there.

Ironically, the following month saw another by-election opportunity at Bridgwater, when Patton was made Lord Advocate in the new Tory government, and so had to stand for re-election, as was the practice then. However, Bagehot declined to stand, due to his unwillingness to allow any electoral malpractice by his supporters; he emphasised that he had wanted his June campaign to be 'pure'.

The full story of the shady dealings at the June by-election emerged 3 years later when there was a Royal Commission into Bridgwater's endemic electoral corruption. Appearing before the inquiry on Wednesday 13 October 1869, its 41st sitting day, Walter admitted that, though he did not participate in any wrongdoing at the June 1866 by-election, his election team did, and he had chosen, following legal advice, to reimburse personally the £800 spent illegally as the only honourable option. His fear of a repetition of this unlawful conduct by his supporters was why he would not stand again at Bridgwater. His evidence appeared to reveal him as being at the very least naïve careless and ignorant, but not intentionally criminal or corrupt. Overall, it must have been a gruelling session for him, though Eliza's very brief diary entry simply stated "Walter gave evidence before the Bridgwater Commissioners who were very civil."

A curious indication of Bagehot's reaction to all this appeared in a letter around that time to Hutton, where he remarked, in an apparent mixture of relief and perhaps smugness: "You will like to hear that my reputation for ability is much raised at Bridgwater since my examination. They say, 'Ah! Mr Bagehot was too many for them. They broke Westropp but they could not break him. They regard it as a kind of skill, independent of fact or truth. 'You'll win if you are clever, and you lose if you are stupid,' is their idea at bottom."

When the inquiry's report was finally published early the following year, it was clearly damning against Bagehot. It stated in reference to that June 1866 by-election, "We find ... that Walter Bagehot and George Patton, Esquires, the candidates, were privy and assenting to some of the corrupt practices extensively prevailing thereat." His name appeared in the accompanying Schedule among a long list of 'bribers' at that election.

Fortunately for Bagehot, this indictment did not seem to have any long-term negative consequences for his career or reputation, and his chroniclers and supporters have tended to gloss over the incident and its outcome.

Final efforts

When it was clear that London University would finally gain its own parliamentary seat under the Reform Act 1867, with its graduates being its electors, renewed efforts were made by Bagehot's friends, especially Hutton, to induce him to put himself forward, as a graduate of the University. Walter seemed to be willing to give it a go, and wrote a letter to Hutton in June of that year intended to be published as his personal 'manifesto'. Unfortunately it contained an attack on Disraeli, accusing him of seeking to woo the newly-enfranchised voters across the country through influence and corruption, which did not endear him to Conservative voters in the University seat.

There followed a year-long bitter and divisive battle for the Liberal nomination, with much invective in the press against Bagehot among others, which threatened to damage his wider reputation. By the summer of 1868 it appeared to come down to a straight fight between Bagehot and the veteran senior former minister, Robert Lowe, who was looking for a more congenial seat than his existing one of Calne in Wiltshire. Bagehot could see the writing on the wall and withdrew from the contest in a letter of 30 July. Sure enough, Lowe not only won the seat but was also appointed as Chancellor of the Exchequer in the incoming Gladstone Government.

In the autumn of 1868, Bagehot, who had been recovering from illness in the Pyrenees, had been approached by two friends to stand for Mid-Somerset in the imminent general election. He declined the offer, due to his health, and later was active in campaigning for the Liberal candidates in the election. However on his return from his convalescence to London in early October he discovered that his supporters had sent a telegram to Gladstone to help secure Bagehot that Mid-Somerset nomination. Highly embarrassed, Walter wrote to Gladstone to distance himself from that unofficial approach: "what the Yeovil people meant by troubling you I cannot think. I hope you were only amused at such an explosion of electioneering zeal."

Finally, in early 1873 Bagehot was approached to stand for nomination as the Liberal candidate in a by-election at Liverpool, but he declined. This marked the practical end of any parliamentary ambitions he may have had for himself, or others on his behalf. For all the times he tipped his toe in parliamentary electoral waters – or was asked to but declined – it remains the case that Bridgwater in 1866 had been his only actual formal candidacy that lasted until polling day itself.

As the wistful remarks in his 1870 Metaphysical Society speech suggest, he had some desire to become an MP (or at least MP for Bridgwater). His failure to do so may have been the first, or at least the most serious, setback in his professional life, inevitably something of a shock to him. However, given the unwelcome episode of the Bribery Commissioner's inquiry into his 1866 Bridgwater foray, perhaps he was also a bit relieved not to have become a full participant in Westminster parliamentary politics. His recognition of his own unsuitability for that world, by describing himself as being "between sizes in politics", indicates an acceptance of that bittersweet truth.

CHAPTER TEN
In his spare time

Bagehot was a very busy man, with his very full professional life in Langport and London, his obligations as a co-executor and co-trustee and his various unsuccessful forays onto the electoral stage. There wasn't much time left for other things. So what did he do in his limited spare time? This chapter provides a brief overview of these various 'non-professional' activities.

However, his family circumstances must always be borne in mind. Throughout his adult life, he and his father had the constant strain of his mother's ill-health to deal with. In one particularly serious fit of insanity in 1866, she broke the windows in the Langport bank. Unable to calm her, his uncle Edward Bagehot and Dr Prankerd, the local doctor, had to commit her to an asylum near Bristol. Walter had to come home from London to be with his father, and to visit his mother. According to Emilie Barrington, his mother's insanity was "the tragedy of his life, the iron that entered into the soul."

Under James Wilson's patronage, and his marriage to Eliza, the eldest daughter, in the late 1850s, he had quickly assumed a de facto senior role within the Wilson family. He was both a 'big brother' to Eliza's sisters, and, following Wilson's death, a substitute 'head of household' for them and their mother. Not only was this exercised through the legal authority he had been granted under James Wilson's will, but also by the sheer force of his personality. Finally, he and Eliza were childless, and while there is virtually nothing on the record about how they felt about it, or how it affected the patterns of their maturer years, it was a relevant factor. While it allowed them more freedom to go about their very varied lives in the 1860s and 1870s, they must have thought about it a lot, especially when in contact with children of the families or friends.

Games and sports

According to his sister-in-law Emilie, "Cup-and-ball was Walter's favourite game. How distinctly I see him now steadying the ball while gazing at it sideways very intently with his large round black eyes, an eye-glass stuck in one. He was thirty-two years of age, but he still had a boy's keen zest in playing certain games."

Card games were a regular feature of Walter's home life. Family dinner parties often ended with games of whist, or occasionally Pope Joan or Commerce, popular games of that era. Matilda, Eliza's extrovert younger sister, taught Walter how to play bezique, a trick-taking game for two players. Having only learned it on 11 September 1869, two days later he and Matilda played it for five hours both before and after dinner. After that Walter often played it with Matilda, and occasionally with Russell, Emilie's husband. He particularly liked playing with Matilda because he thought she had "a true gambler's spirit...it was of no use to play with people who were callous as to whether their cards were good or bad". Eliza didn't seem to play it. Rather poignantly, Eliza records that despite being gravely ill, Walter played cribbage with his aunt on the afternoon before he died.

Walter and Eliza often played battledore and shuttlecock together. A precursor of badminton, it was played without a net. The object was to keep the shuttlecock off the ground as long as possible, using a flat bat. The diaries only ever record Walter and Eliza playing it together, not with anyone else. It could be played indoors as well as outdoors, but it seems that they usually played it inside, when the weather was wet.

Eliza & Walter playing battledore & shuttlecock

Billiards was played when he visited the Wilsons at Claverton Manor, and croquet was enjoyed at Herd's Hill, but what Walter really loved was riding and hunting, and he usually kept his own horse. In 1843, when his poor health had forced him to miss the autumn term at UCL, he went home to Herd's Hill to recuperate. A horse, "the grey" mentioned in his letters, was acquired, and, much to his enjoyment, he rode and hunted with it during the five months he was at home. A few years after he had moved back to Langport full time in 1852, he started keeping a pack of harriers with his cousin, Vincent Wood. In time these became known as the Langport Harriers, and when Vincent announced his intention to discontinue them at the end of the 1860 season, there was an outcry locally. After a public meeting, Samuel Pitman agreed to become the new Master, and they carried on.

Walter never bought a horse without first consulting his uncle, John Stuckey Reynolds, who was a first-rate judge of a horse. In January 1864 he bought a grey cob in Exeter. He took it to London with him, but a few weeks later it threw him. Later that year, while he and Eliza were staying at Great Marlow, his ponies, Charlie and Fanny, were brought from Langport, and his horse Plaything from London. Riding gave him pleasure, relaxation, and perhaps time to think. He confessed as much to Eliza in a letter in November 1857: "I thought of you all day yesterday under pretence of a day's hunt with very little sport. ... There is *no* time for quiet reflection like the intervals of a hunt..."

Social life – entertaining and visiting

As a child in Langport Walter's social life naturally revolved around his family and their circle of friends. His 'Uncle Stuckey' – Vincent Stuckey, head of the successful Stuckey's Bank - lived at Hill House, opposite All Saints' Church, and he also had a house in Sloane Square in London, where Walter's mother used to visit occasionally. There were Sunday afternoon levees at Hill House, when the Bagehots often visited after attending church.

Originally built as Hill House, home of Vincent Stuckey, head of Stuckey's Bank, across the road from All Saints' Church, Langport

Once he moved to school in Bristol, however, Walter's horizons began to expand. There he spent most of his free time talking about scientific subjects with Dr Prichard, who taught a course at his school, and Alfred Estlin, both of whom were relatives through his mother's first marriage to Joseph Prior Estlin. He also developed friendships there which lasted for the rest of his life.

In the early 1850s, when Walter had moved back home to Langport, his mother would often host long-drawn out social occasions. Emilie Barrington gives a detailed account of what they were like:

> There were days when visitors, relations, or old friends from the neighbourhood would arrive at Herd's Hill at noon, and talk till, and through luncheon - talk till five o'clock tea - talk till dinner and through dinner. There was a pause after dinner for tea, cards and music; then the tray would appear, wine, sandwiches and cake - then family prayers, then a little more talk, and the departure of the guests would not take place long before midnight. What the talk was about it is impossible to recall, but the miracle remains, that, after nearly twelve hours of talking, the company - guests and hosts - did not become either dull, weary or sleepy.

However, Walter's marriage to Eliza Wilson catapulted him into a higher level of social life. The six Wilson sisters welcomed Bagehot straight away and treated him like the brother they never had. More significantly, their father James was a Government Minister and founder of *The Economist*, which drew him into the political arena and the metropolitan social scene. After James's death and his assumption of the editorship of *The Economist*, Walter and Eliza spent much more time in London. Here they enjoyed attending – and giving - regular dinner parties with family, friends and political contacts. Walter seemed to enjoy socialising most of all when it involved debate or discussion about topics that interested him. He did not appear at Eliza's regular afternoon tea-parties, and often seemed to prefer dining at a club instead of at home with Eliza.

Some dinner parties were more important than others. Eliza records a notable one on 1 April 1859:

> Political dinner at home to introduce Walter to some admirers of his pamphlet on Reform: Lord Gray, Lord Granville, William Gladstone, Lord Cardwell, Bouverie, Thackeray, Sir S C Lewis, Sir Richard Bethell.

Another on 6 May 1872:

> We were asked to an evening party at Lady Waldegrave's to meet the King of the Belgians.

Some, particularly those in Langport, were arranged for business reasons, such as what the diaries describe as 'bankers dinner parties'. Others, especially in London, were simply with or at the homes of family or friends.

Walter spent a lot of time with his brother-in-law W R Greg (Julia Wilson's husband), who wrote on political subjects. Emilie recalls that "they had mutual friends notable in the literary and political world, and pleasant dinner parties took place at both houses, remarkable for the intellectual distinction of the guests." He also paid regular visits to politicians such as Lord Carnarvon at his home at Highclere, and the banker Sir John Lubbock (Lord Avebury) at High Elms, Farnborough, often staying overnight.

Walter seemed happier in familiar company – he was less comfortable in large gatherings, as he wrote to one of his sisters-in-law, "It is inconceivable to me to like to see many people and even to speak to them. Every new person you know is an intellectual burden because you may see them again, and must be able to recognise and willing to converse with them." Eliza notes one social occasion which – unusually for him - Walter seemed to have enjoyed, a ball given by her mother, Elizabeth Wilson: "I think our ball went off we... It was very full (nearly 300 people) and spirited, and we kept it up till half-past three. Walter really enjoyed it, and behaved quite nicely, not retiring once till he slipped away to bed at a quarter before three." Perhaps he was showing off his waltzing, which he had learned. not entirely successfully, during his stay in Paris.

In those days, Eliza, as the woman of the house, would have had the major role in most matters domestic, such as entertaining. She would probably also have been ma n.y responsible for the more general running of their homes, especially in the hir ng and firing of their servants, as her diaries attest, though Walter may have had some role regarding those who more directly served him (including drivers). The diaries also show that they shared the chores of doing their financial accounts.

Clubs and societies

Bagehot enjoyed going to London clubs for many reasons. Sometimes he needed a place to work away from other distractions. More often he would have dinner there with friends, and use a club as a social centre to meet new and interesting contacts who might provide him with useful information. Others provided a more intellectual rather than recreational forum.

The three more 'social' clubs he belonged to were Brooks's, the Athenaeum, and the Wyndham (or Windham) Club. In 1869 he was elected to the exclusive Brooks's Club. His proposer was Lord Granville, Gladstone's Colonial Secretary. Bagehot was elected to the prestigious Athenaeum in 1875. "The committee elected me yesterday at the Athenaeum quite cheerfully", he wrote to his wife on 14 April. "By the rule they can only elect nine persons a year and those 'who have eminence in Science, Literature, the Arts or for public services.' I wonder in which *my* eminence is." He and his friend, and fellow-member, Richard Holt Hutton often relaxed there over a game of chess.

The lobby of the Athenaeum Club in Victorian times

73

The Wyndham Club's object was "to secure a convenient and agreeable place of meeting for a society of gentlemen, all connected with each other by a common bond of literary or personal acquaintance." Its premises were in St James' Square, conveniently next door to the London Library.

There were other clubs where he went for more intellectual stimulation, such as the Royal Statistical Society, of which his colleague at *The Economist*, William Newmarch, was later President. He was elected a Fellow in January 1864, and served as a member of its Council for the 1869-70 session. He enjoyed places where he could join in discussion and debate, such as the Century Club (a forerunner of the National Liberal Club), which included many members who were writers like himself.

Bagehot was elected to a more influential body, the Political Economy Club, in 1864. Limited to 35 members, it was composed mainly of businessmen, politicians, civil servants and professional economists. Members could propose a question for discussion, related to a particular economic theory or policy, which was then debated during an evening banquet dinner. For example, on 3 March 1875 Bagehot proposed a question on the tendency of interest rates to rise. One of the members who took part in the ensuing discussion was W E Gladstone.

Some years later John Macdonald, the first Prime Minister of Canada, but then Leader of the Opposition, recalled a dinner he had enjoyed at the Political Economy Club. Speaking during a parliamentary debate in the Canadian House of Commons on 11 April 1878, he said,

> I shall first quote an author who has been quoted again and again, Mr Bagehot, whose lamented decease struck England with sorrow, especially all political constitutionalists, for he was considered the authority of the day on constitutional law. If I am permitted in this argument to relate a little anecdote, I would do so with reference to this gentleman. This book from which I quote was in the first place published in the *Fortnightly Review*. I had read some of the numbers before I went to England in 1865, and I was dining with the 'Political Economy Club' of London, of which the hon. The Premier is a member, when in the course of a conversation on political economical matters with a gentleman who sat near me, I said: "I have been very much struck with some articles in the *Fortnightly Review* on the English Constitution. It seems to me that they give the only true picture of the British Constitution as it now exists. They are written by one Mr Bagehot." He said: "I am very glad you like them because I am Mr Bagehot." From that time an acquaintance grew up between us, which only ceased with his lamented death.

Macdonald made another trip to London in 1866-7, during which he led the London Conference on the proposed Canadian confederation and married his second wife, Agnes. They were both guests of honour at a dinner at the Bagehot's London home on 29 March 1867, the very day on which the British North America Act was given the Royal Assent, creating the foundation of Canada's constitution.

Bagehot was one of the earliest members of the Metaphysical Society, formed in 1869 with the object of debating topics related to science and religion. Membership was by invitation only, and was small but distinguished. Bagehot presented a number of papers and greatly enjoyed the stimulating discussions that took place at the Society. His first paper, given on 13 December 1870, was called 'On the emotion of conviction'. In it he cited himself as an example of utterly irrational conviction, in his belief that he would one day be the Member of Parliament for Bridgwater, despite having been defeated when he stood there at a by-election several years earlier.

'Culture'

Bagehot inherited from his parents a lifelong love of literature and reading in general. He preferred reading to any other form of cultural recreation. Unlike Eliza, who was passionate about music and theatre, he disliked the theatre, thought music was an annoying distraction (though Emilie tried to convert him in his final months), and got no pleasure from art. Poetry, however, was an abiding love, and he often read it aloud. He wrote at least one poem himself, about the Greek legend of Orithyia, who fell in love with the North wind, which he sent to Eliza several years later during their courtship. What Eliza thought of it has not survived. Bagehot's engagement present to Eliza was a set of the poetry of Wordsworth, Shelley and Keats, bound in red calf. He studied poetry and wrote essays about poets, believing poetry to be "a deep thing, a teaching thing, the most surely and wisely elevating of all human things."

Aside from poetry, he enjoyed reading works of philosophical and religious speculation, as well as literary classics. Walter Scott was one of his favourite authors, and Eliza brought a new copy of *Rob Roy* for him to read in his last hours at Herd's Hill.

Travel and holidays

As a young man, Bagehot enjoyed travelling, particularly to Europe. In July 1844, at the age of 18, his 'Aunt Reynolds' (his father's older sister, Mary Anne) and her husband, John Stuckey Reynolds, took him on his first foreign trip. Bagehot kept a 'travel journal', in which he recorded with enthusiasm their sightseeing visits in Bruges, and around Germany and Switzerland. In 1851-2 he spent several months in Paris, enjoying French society, although he was caught up in the coup d'état, about which he famously wrote.

His wife, Eliza, also loved to travel, and they went to France several times in the early years of their marriage, although the West Country was a favourite destination for short trips. They spent their honeymoon travelling around Devon and Cornwall. After they had seen James Wilson and his party depart on their journey to India in 1859, Walter and Eliza, together with her sisters Julia and Emilie, took a break on the Isle of Wight.

In September 1867 they toured the North Devon coast, staying at Westward Ho! and Barnstaple. Eliza 'had a donkey', and she and Walter went along the coast to Clovelly.

The Westward Ho! Hotel in 1864

Walter and Eliza often went to seaside resorts, where they hoped that the fresh air would improve their health. However, as Bagehot's responsibilities increased, he came to view holidays differently. They became opportunities to get away from his daily life and write in peace. According to Emilie Barrington, "When Bagehot's mind was engaged on any special piece of writing he did not travel abroad but chose some attractive place in England where he could write at leisure during the autumn holiday."

Even when he was ill, or recuperating from illness, he would still be 'at work' writing articles or correcting proofs. On 24 March 1868, for example, he and Eliza were on their way to Lyme Regis so that he could enjoy the restorative sea air. Eliza's diary records this: "We left Langport 3 for Lyme Regis, stopped at Axminster for tea and to write letters, sending off revise of second number Physics and Politics for Fortnightly Review." Three days later: "27th March. We drove to Axminster before lunch to send the Money Article for Economist."

There were some periods of pure relaxation for Walter when they were away from home. He enjoyed riding, sometimes having his horse brought from London for him to ride. When they stayed at Great Marlow he and Eliza enjoyed rowing on the Thames, although whether they actually took the oars themselves is not clear.

Schlangenbad, a health resort in Germany where Eliza liked to take the waters

Walter and Eliza were in the habit of having an autumn break on the Continent every year, lasting four or five weeks or more. For example, in September-October 1871 they spent a month in Europe, mostly in Germany, an interesting choice in the aftermath of the Franco-Prussian war. It did not, however, get off to a good start. After crossing the Channel they stayed overnight at the Hotel de l'Europe in Brussels, only to find in the morning that they had been robbed during the night. Eliza wrote, "Awoke about 7 to find our bedroom door ajar & my watch, chain, purse & all the gold pieces from Walter's money stolen. We sent for the landlady at once, who got a police inspector directly. He searched the hotel & the servants, but found nothing."

They carried on until they reached Schlangenbad, a spa where Eliza liked to take the waters. Even here Walter was busy. The first thing he did when they arrived at the Hotel was to go to the library and take out a subscription. Later in their stay he took a train to

Frankfurt for a few days, met four of the principal bankers there and then wrote an article on German finances for *The Economist*.

In the following year Eliza went to Schlangenbac without Walter, taking Mrs Pretty as a maid and companion. Walter had intended to join her, but fell ill and did not go. In 1873 they both enjoyed an extended stay in Europe, and in 1874 they spent several weeks in France. The next two years' autumn breaks were taken closer to home, either in Devon or in Surrey, while Walter was working on his book on political economy. Their last trip together, in September 1875, took in Ascot and Bagshot. However, their stay was interrupted by Walter going to London several times on business for a day, and to Langport for several days. It was not surprising, therefore, that on one occasion he fell asleep on the train, missed his stop and had to take a fly to get home to London.

His early opinion of holidays was truly borne out by his later experiences: "As to holidays, it is one of the lessons of life to learn to be independent of them."

Family duties

Shortly before James Wilson's departure to India in October 1859, Walter was at his side. In a letter to Eliza, he wrote: "I sat up late last night with your father about his will which was a cheerful topic". He was made an executor, together with Walter, John and George Wilson, James's brothers. Little did they know that they would be called on to act just a year later.

After James Wilson's death Walter became adviser and virtual father-figure to Eliza's five sisters. For example, on 23 November 1867 Russell Barrington, who had become engaged to Emilie, talked to Walter about his prospects. He did not have independent means, and was evidently persuaded that he ought to improve his position. Eliza's diary records that two days later, "Walter saw Mr Barrington in City morning & found he had arranged to have a Western branch of Mr Day's business". This probably refers to T H Day, who was a director of the Provincial Banking Corporation. His father gave his approval, and then discussed matters with Walter. Eliza writes, "Mr Barrington's father came at 10 to have a business talk with Walter about the engagement & settlements etc."

When it came to their wedding on 1 July the following year, Walter 'fathered' it, and made all the arrangements. He did the same for Emilie's sister Zoë, who had married Orby Shipley a month earlier.

Civic duties

Bagehot was sworn in as a magistrate for Somerset on 2 January 1861, and took his duties very seriously. He attended both Quarter Sessions and Petty Sessions regularly while he was based in Clevedon. Even after he had moved to London he attended when he could, often combining it with meetings of the Directors of Stuckey's Bank and a visit to his parents in Langport. As ever, he came up with new ideas whenever an opportunity arose. In 1865 he proposed a motion to his fellow Justices that they should set up a committee to consider whether to adopt the prison discipline regime that had just been introduced in Hampshire.

Eliza's diaries record that he was invited (as a magistrate) to join the procession at the opening of the Clifton Bridge on 8 December 1864, but he declined. It was probably wise not to risk his health. He was summoned for jury service in February 1866, but was not well, and so he sent in a medical certificate and was exempted.

The annual meeting of Langport Corporation held on 1 November 1872 saw Bagehot elected and sworn in as Deputy Recorder of Langport. In the evening he attended the traditional dinner given by the outgoing Portreeve (mayor), his cousin Joseph Barnes Bagehot. His duties do not seem to have been onerous, although he attended official engagements as part of the Corporation.

Community life

Langport Town Hall, with its distinctive arches, Bow Street

When he was back in Langport, Bagehot occasionally took part in local events. On 27 August 1861, when the Somersetshire Archaeological and Natural History Society held its 13th annual congress in Langport, meeting in the newly renovated Town Hall, Bagehot was due to present a paper about the Battle of Langport. His parents and his wife came to the meeting to hear him speak. Unfortunately, a previous speaker had already given an account of the battle, so Walter just had to make a few remarks instead of a full speech. Even so, they proved controversial, contending that the Cavaliers had been swept completely out of the West of England by that battle. This offended the Rev. F Warre, who complained that Bagehot was treading on tender ground. He had evidently lost nine out of twelve Cavalier ancestors, and "felt rather keenly on this point."

Two months later the Langport Literary and Scientific Institution opened its doors. Its purpose was to provide entertainment for the leisure hours of the young men of the town to aid their 'social and mental improvement'. In February of the following year Bagehot gave a lecture to the members of the Institution on "the sort of reading most suitable for persons engaged in active occupations." He recommended reading newspapers and books on biography and history, and avoiding novels "of a very trashy description." His final advice was simply "read something." According to a report in the

Wells Journal of 8 February 1862, he caused 'great mirth and entertainment by interspersing a number of exceedingly droll anecdotes'.

House-hunting

Until his marriage, Walter had either lived at home or lodged with other people, so his earliest experience of house-hunting was to find his first married home. He and Eliza were due to be married in April 1858, but Eliza was still in Edinburgh, having her head 'rubbed' in an attempt to cure her headaches, so Walter had to conduct what he called his 'mansion-chase' on his own, fitting it around his work at the Bristol Bank. It was obviously a strain, as he told Eliza on 21 January 1858, "Houses and banking together are too much for *any* mind."

Ideally it would be somewhere that would provide convenient access to the two families' homes in Langport and Claverton, and for his banking duties, especially in Langport and Bristol. On 20 January 1858 he reported that he had a list of four possible houses to see. The last one, in Clevedon, he described as "A most scrumptious mansion built as a summer residence by Sir A Elton, called Bella Vista from its magnificent view, to be vacant in April, but too good for us, I fear." It sounded unattainable: "The description of Bella Vista is ravishing but its utility is only in showing what we are not rich enough to have." Nevertheless, after some discussion about economies they might make, they decided to take it, despite Eliza not having seen it. They took possession on 20 April 1858, changing its name to The Arches.

It was a very different story 17 years later, when they were looking for a permanent home in London. August 1875 saw a frenzy of house-hunting, using Elsworth & Knighton, the leading house agents in South Kensington. Eliza, sometimes accompanied by one of her sisters, looked for suitable places, and then she and Walter viewed them together. These diary entries give a flavour of their hunt:

> Saturday 7 August: Walter walked to Elsworth's morning & round the neighbourhood to look for houses. We drove together afternoon & looked at 43 Prince's Gardens, 8, 31 Queen's Gate Place & 40 Queen's Gate Gardens.

> Thursday 12 August: Walter came home to lunch & go with me to see 21 & 14 Queen's Gate Gardens & we went to Elsworth's office about them.

> Saturday 14 August: Mr Elsworth came & drew up Walter's offer for 21 Queen's Gate Gardens, which he took to give to Mr Stapleton.

> Thursday 19 August: Mr Elsworth called morning & we talked over the houses. Walter & I went deliberately over 8 Queen's Gate Place & 21 Queen's Gate Gardens afternoon. Mr Stapleton had declined £8250 for the latter.

After several other abortive offers, they eventually secured 8 Queen's Gate Place on 8th September. This was to be their last home together.

Furnishing their homes

Having found their properties, they would set about turning them into homes. This involved furnishing them and sometimes altering them to their taste. This didn't apply just to their London homes, but also to Herd's Hill, where they spent large parts of each year. They usually shopped at the best establishments in London, such as Heal's and Harvey Nichols. The diaries make very little mention of Walter joining Eliza in her shopping expeditions, except when it came to buying things for Herd's Hill. In some cases, these purchases were then delivered to 'the bridge', meaning Stuckey & Bagehot's warehouse at Great Bow Bridge in Langport.

Herd's Hill as it would have looked when Walter lived there

Early in 1871, for example, alterations were being made to the library at Herd's Hill, presumably for Walter's benefit:

Friday 3 March 1871
Mr Edward Bagehot called to tell us that Walter's library cannot be enlarged, but a recess could be made

Tuesday 14 March
Mr Edward Bagehot met Mr Davis the builder here afternoon & Walter & they arranged about the recess in his Library & the new cellar stairs.

They then bought various items for his library, including 'yellow Utrecht velvet curtains' from William Morris's, two Persian rugs and a fender. William Morris's firm became a favourite source for quality décor, and they often dealt with his manager, George Wardle. Walter was fully engaged in these expeditions, particularly enjoying his discussions with Morris about poetry as well as furnishings. In a letter to Emilie in December 1875, Walter remarked, "Wardle is doing most of the house, but the great man himself, William Morris, is composing the drawing-room, as he would an ode."

William Morris and Walter Bagehot discussing poetry – and curtains!

They were also drawn to the work of William De Morgan, son of Professor Augustus De Morgan, who had taught Walter mathematics at UCL. Both William De Morgan tiles and William Morris wallpapers were bought for Herd's Hill as well as for Queen's Gate Place.

The rest of the furnishings were left to Eliza to search out, usually with her sister Emilie. For example, on 24 January 1876 she bought a venetian mirror, a pair of sconces and a pair of cloisonné flower pots at Edwards & Roberts. The following week they purchased 'an old Crown Derby dinner service and a pair of old Nuremberg iron & brass lamps'. Later, they bought 'some iron work, a pair of sconces, 5 Rhodian plates & a cabinet'. On Wednesday 8 March, rather surprisingly, Eliza recorded that she drove to Leicester Square and Lambeth and 'ransacked old furniture shops'. Walter was busy at work, and did not accompany them.

The tale of the curtains was rather a sad one. William Morris was 'composing' a very beautiful blue damask silk for the curtains and furniture of their drawing rooms, but this seemed to take an inordinate length of time. Walter said, "They bring me sample-threads every two or three months but the curtains don't come." In fact, Walter never saw those curtains, which still hadn't arrived when he left Queen's Gate Place on his last journey to Herd's Hill.

CHAPTER ELEVEN

Final days

His death

On Sunday 18 March 1877, while he was working in the study of his London home at 8 Queen's Gate Place, high up on the third floor, and, he believed, "out of the fuss of the front door," he caught a new cold which took hold. Though the cold winds were coming through the barely-protected windows – they were still awaiting the delivery of new curtains ordered from the firm of William Morris – Walter had refused to take steps to keep warm and would lie full-length on a sofa under the windows, rather than by the fire. His wife, Eliza, called in his doctor.

His sister-in-law, Emilie Barrington, who, with her husband and young son, had been staying at the Bagehots since February, wrote that "during his last days he appears to have thought seriously of his state of health" and reported a friend of his as recalling that, at that time, Walter had told a member of *The Economist* staff "that he did not think he should get over his cold." She also wrote that, during his final week in London, "he left his bed and, going up to his study, made his will."

Walter refused to stay in bed because he had promised his father he would spend Easter at Herd's Hill. He may also have had meetings to attend there, as there is a reference (discussed below) to a meeting on 'Bridge business' on 22 March, though it is not known whether he had planned to attend.

Emilie recalled their departure from their house: "When he started he was clearly ill. My sister and I were in the carriage and my husband was on the pavement to see us off. Before Walter got into the carriage, he turned to him to say goodbye. But there was no accustomed quaint word of fun, no life. The lamp was already burning low. For the first time the boyish spirit seemed extinguished."

He and Eliza left from Waterloo Station on the afternoon of Tuesday 20 March, which was the last time Emilie saw him alive. The original plan to depart that morning had been changed as Walter had agreed to attend The Atheneum to vote for a friend of Eliza's as a member. It was a raw, wintry day, and matters were not helped by a long delay between trains at Yeovil Station.

Walter was very ill when he arrived at Herd's Hill. He was attended by doctors, and Eliza recorded that on Wednesday 21st he was "very ill ... had a bad night & sat up most of it." There was no improvement the following day: "He was worse evening & did not sleep after 12. He changed rooms for the night."

Though he managed, on Friday 23rd, to play cribbage with his aunt – Emma Michell (his father's youngest sister) - who was nursing him, he was diagnosed as having congestion of the lung. Eliza noted that the doctor saw him twice and told her that "Walter was dangerously, but not hopelessly ill."

It is not known whether he did, or tried to do, any work while in bed at Herd's Hill. He did write a letter in pencil to Hutton on the 21st. Several days previously Hutton had said to his friend that he thought he was "looking so young and well" that he could hardly believe they were contemporaries. Walter, presumably seeing the unintended irony of his friend's remarks, wrote, "I think you must have had the evil eye when you complimented me on my appearance. Ever since, I have been sickening, and am now in bed with a severe attack on the lungs."

Mention has already been made of two matters on Thursday 22 March that were business-related. The first was that his friend and former assistant at *The Economist* Robert Giffen, had written to him on that day about some background research for a proposed article on bankruptcy, and, prompted by a telegram Bagehot had sent him, remarked, "I hope you have not been overdoing your work lately, as it is so easy to do.' The other was the visit, as recorded in Eliza's diary, of two of his relatives involved in the 'Bridge' mercantile businesses, Watson and Barnes Bagehot, who saw him "about the Bridge meeting while it was going on."

The entry for Saturday 24 March is the longest of any entry in her diary. It is recorded on a sheet of paper inserted into the 24 March page. It seemed that, despite his obvious serious condition, Walter's final deterioration was something of a shock, as one biographer remarked: "[s]till there is a note of clammy incredulity as Eliza writes of his death – so terrible in its suddenness."

Walter slightly better after 5am. I breakfasted with him and his aunt left the sofa and went to bed. I spent morning on the bed by him and cut a new copy of Rob Roy for him to read. Mr Brooks came at 9 and 2 and was satisfied that his bronchitis was rather better. Walter spoke often of his extreme weakness increasing as the day advanced. I spent afternoon behind curtain so as not to disturb him and wrote to Mr Batten and Mr Wm Coles for him. About 4 he asked me if I "had been down to the parlour today"; he exerted himself with his pillows and would not let me help him, saying, "let me have my own fidgets", but called me to him and soon fell fast asleep across the bed – breathing very loud and hard. This gradually quieted and I went down and told his father and aunt the change for the better had come – then knelt by him to count his pulse at 5:25 but had my own; – while I counted, a little purple came on his lips and he became still and white. I called his aunt – then poured brandy down his throat. They said it was of no use and I knew he was gone.

He was just 51 years old.

Understandably, Eliza was clearly in a state of shock in the immediate aftermath of her husband's death. Her diary for the day after, Sunday 25th, is simple, yet (unusually for her diary entries) with hints of emotion: "Sweet morning – birds singing when I woke. Only slept from 5 to 6 o'clock am. ... Knight made two photographs. I went to Mr Bagehot at 12, who cried much. Mr Edward came to my room afternoon. I wrote letters all day. Watson called afternoon & saw Walter." Unfortunately no deathbed photographs survive.

Portrait of Eliza in later life

84

The entry for Monday shows her ever more drawn into the practicalities of the situation, despite her grief: "Only slept from 12 to 2 am. Mr Edward Bagehot consulted me as to arrangements for dear Walter's funeral. Mr Estlin came & Mr Bagehot altered his will, putting me in Walter's place. Mr Bagehot told me to write for Walter's will." Tuesday was blank in her diary, but on the following day, the practical arrangements continued: "Received Walter's will from Mr Primet & showed it to Mr Bagehot. Slept afternoon & was refreshed. Julia, Emilie & Russell came by Yeovil before 8. I went to north rooms to see them & to dine. They brought my weeds."

According to Emilie, who had returned with her family to their Wimbledon home on Tuesday 20th, there had been rumours of Walter's death in that Sunday's papers, which her servants had seen but didn't report them to her, as they may have thought they referred to Walter's father, not Walter himself. Having only discovered conclusively about Walter's death on the Monday morning, she went with her husband, Russell, and her sister, Julia Greg, to Langport for the funeral.

One bizarre episode shortly after his death was the appearance in early June in some provincial newspapers of the following item: "No one appears to have mentioned the fact that the late Mr. Walter Bagehot died literally in harness. He was sitting in his chair writing an article at the time of his seizure." This extraordinary claim is not mentioned at all in any reputable source, including Eliza's diaries, in any form that could have given rise to the claim. Its provenance is unknown, and in the absence of any supporting information, must be regarded as an example of late 19th century 'fake news'.

His funeral

Walter's funeral took place on 29 March 1877 (Maundy Thursday). The main sources for the events are Eliza's diary, and the reports in the *Langport Herald* of Saturday 31 March and Saturday 7 April. According to the diary entry for 26 March, Edward Bagehot, Walter's uncle, consulted her about the funeral arrangements. Interestingly, there seems to be no reference in the diary or press report of Thomas attending his son's funeral, though other family members are listed, which may suggest that he was unable to be there, presumably on health grounds.

The cortège of the hearse and four mourning coaches left Herd's Hill just after midday – Eliza's diary has it as 12 noon, while the *Herald* states it was 1pm – and travelled to St Mary's Church, Huish Episcopi. Emilie wrote that a photograph had been taken of "the simple procession as it passed through the street of the little ancient Langport town, the gig of the undertaker leading the way, which was the local fashion in those days." Sadly the photograph has not survived.

St Mary's Church, Huish Episcopi, where Walter's funeral service was held

Huish Church was the venue, as the usual family church, All Saints on Langport Hill, was closed for restoration. The service was performed by the Huish vicar, Rev Edward Henslowe. The funeral party then proceeded to All Saints' Church, where the coffin was interred in the family vault in the south-eastern corner of the churchyard, after Eliza's sisters laid a cross and wreaths of white flowers on it. Rev Henslowe again presided, and various family servants acted as bearers and pall-bearers.

According to the *Langport Herald*, "The inhabitants [of Langport] generally testified their respect towards the deceased gentleman by closing their shops during the afternoon."

Three days later, on the afternoon of Easter Sunday, before a large congregation, Rev Henslowe gave a funeral sermon at Huish Church, based on Matthew xxiv, 44. "Be ye also ready, for in such an hour as ye think not. The Son of Man cometh." He also referred to the "immeasurable loss" of Walter's death, saying that it required abler hands than his to do justice to the great talents of the deceased. All deeply sympathised with "his aged father in his bitter grief at the loss of such a promising son." It was noted in both Eliza's diary and the *Herald* report that the service was attended by members of Langport Corporation, in their official robes and preceded by the sergeant-at-mace, with the symbol of office draped in black. Walter had been the Corporation's Deputy Recorder since 1872, and the Corporation formally recorded a fine tribute in the minutes of its 26 May meeting.

His will

Walter wrote a will which, though it was undated, was stated on the existing Inland Revenue 'office copy' (drawn up as a copy for death duty purposes; there being no surviving manuscript or original copy of it) as having been executed in 1872. Whether this is the same will that Emilie Barrington claimed he wrote in his final days in London in 1877 is not known. It was proved in London on 5 May 1877 by the oath of Eliza as widow, relict and sole executrix to whom administration was granted. Her oath may actually have been given earlier, as her diary entry for 25 April noted that, while at Herd's Hill, "Mr Estlin brought Mr Parsons to swear me to affidavit for probate duty at 11 o'clock." The *Langport Herald* of 9 June reported that the personal estate was sworn as under £40,000.

In his transcription of that 'office copy' for the *Collected Works* Stevas named the two witnesses to the will as G B Primel and T W Tegelmeir.   The first-named was actually George Banbury Primet (1817-1899), who is described in the 1871 Census as being born in Hackney, married and residing in Highbury, Islington, and whose occupation was bank manager. He was the person mentioned as sending Walter's will to Eliza on the Wednesday after his death. This may perhaps suggest he was connected to Bagehot through Stuckey's Bank. One coincidental fact is that his wife, Elizabeth, whom he married in October 1845 in Wilton, near Taunton, Somerset, was the daughter of Richard Carver, the architect of Herd's Hill. Nothing further is known of T W Tegelmeier.

The terms of the will itself were quite brief. He bequeathed all shares, estates and other securities, including those nominally in his name only, that he held on behalf of Stuckey's Banking Company or the estate of James Wilson, back to these entities. Other than a bequest of £1000 ("or any larger sum which he may owe me at the time of my death") to his cousin Watson Bagehot, everything else went to his wife, Eliza, who was appointed sole executrix.

All earlier wills and codicils were revoked, and this was declared to be his last will. Given its unusual aspects, especially its brevity and it being undated, the question arises whether there ever was a later will. In her biography Emilie Barrington is quite clear that he did write a will just before his death: "Another sign that he thought his life precarious showed itself in the fact that one night, during the last week he was in London, he left his bed and, going up to his study, made his will." This was also repeated in Alastair Buchan's 1959 biography, *The Spare Chancellor*, but Stevas dismissed that as "mistaken – no source is given for this statement", notwithstanding the clear Emilie Barrington claim. If such a later will was ever made, it has yet to be found.

Initial tributes and reaction

Walter died on a Saturday, publication day for *The Economist*, so the 24 March issue came out as normal, oblivious to the momentous events in rural Somerset. The following issue, on the 31st, had a black border round its front page and a fulsome tribute from Hutton. Eliza's diary records that the family had hurriedly put together something to go in the paper, written by Bagehot's brother-in-law, and former senior officer at the paper, William Rathbone Greg, and looked over by the others. However, on the 30th, Good Friday, (and thereby cutting it very fine to get anything in before printing), when Russell Barrington (Emilie's husband) took it up to London, he "found that Mr Hutton had written a much better one which was used."

The unexpectedness of Walter's death, on a Saturday in faraway Langport, first reported inconclusively in some Sunday papers, probably accounted for there being initially only fairly brief obituaries in the weekday papers, such as that Tuesday's *Times*. However, more substantial obituaries and tributes soon followed in the national and local press – including of course, the *Langport Herald* - in addition to the extensive and heartfelt one by Hutton in *The Economist*. The major journals, including those which had carried his work in the past, also paid their respects, as well as some of the more specialised media such as the *Bankers Magazine*. Gradually tributes came from further afield, including Europe, Australia and America. A privately published collection of obituaries and tributes was prepared in 1878, entitled *Walter Bagehot: In Memoriam*.

Bodies to which Bagehot was connected also recorded their appreciation of him, from Stuckey's Bank to Langport Corporation to University College London. Even the Government itself joined in, in the person of the Chancellor of the Exchequer, Sir Stafford Northcote, during his Budget speech in the House of Commons on 12 April – a rare honour, indeed. Of the letters that Eliza and her family received, the most notable was a fulsome and personal one from William Gladstone on 12 June to Walter's widow.

Stafford Northcote, Chancellor of the Exchequer

A letter dated 6 April from his brother-in-law W R Greg, responding to condolences from Lady Derby, probably best expressed the Wilson family reaction to Walter's death: "But he was quite a unique man, as irreplaceable in private life as he was universally felt to be in public. ... The family all loved him and leaned upon him as he deserved, and he was the trustee, guardian, and executor of us all." Eliza's own reaction, characteristically, is not made explicit in her diaries, but her grief and loss can clearly be read between the lines.

Emilie Barrington's biography describes the initial reaction among the Bagehot family, especially that of Walter's only surviving parent, his father, who by then was deaf and rather a recluse. She recorded that it was only due to the outpourings of sympathy and appreciation that followed his son's death, that he finally realised how famous and respected he was: "I should never have known how great a man Walter was, had I not survived him."

CHAPTER TWELVE

Bagehot the person

To have a sense of what Bagehot was like throughout his relatively short life depends on images and the descriptions of others and of himself. Unfortunately, all surviving images of him are derived from one unique source, a portrait photograph taken of him in 1864, when he was around 38 years of age.

This places almost total reliance on what descriptions survive of him, whether contemporary, or, more common, based on recollection, mainly by family, friends and admirers, some of which was undertaken as reminiscences or tributes in obituaries, biographies and the like. Such descriptions must be regarded, to some degree, as subjective and even a touch 'rose-tinted.' Some of these people may well have had access to the various images, whether photographs, paintings or drawings, that are mentioned as having been taken of him during his life, but which are now lost. Frustratingly, but all too typically, his wife's diaries have little overtly descriptive or subjective about him as a person, simply reporting his actions day by day.

What did he look like?

The 1864 source image shows a black-and-white left profile face and upper body of an early middle-aged man in mid-19th century dress, and all descriptions of his appearance must be judged against that image or extrapolations of it, both backwards to his childhood, adolescence and young adulthood, and forwards to his middle age.

A copy of the photograph taken in 1864

The overall description by his most comprehensive biographer, Norman St John-Stevas, based on that image, is a convenient starting-point, "The head is noble: the face strong, highly individual, with delicate, chiselled and energetic nose, and suffused with a controlled, semi-suppressed vivacity. The hair and beard are at once luxuriant and fine."

Several descriptions refer to a florid complexion, and his sister-in-law and biographer, Emilie Barrington, who knew him over his last two decades, wrote of "a very fine skin, very white near where the hair started, and a high colour - what might be called a hectic colour - concentrated on the cheek bones, as you often see it in the West country." His face was remarkably expressive, with references to "the play of facial muscle" as a young child, and "a countenance of remarkable vivacity" when a schoolboy in his early teens. A friend from student days onwards referred to him having "something of good-natured mockery in his glance, and his face reflected that habitual reserve of judgment which has been called "detachment of mind." Perhaps some viewers, looking at the 1864 image, may see hints of an enigmatic 'Mona Lisa smile'.

For variety, some sketches have reversed the pose in the original photograph

The dark, thick hair is a striking feature, described even in his early years as an "overhanging thatch of black hair". Bagehot described himself in an 1858 letter to Eliza as "*that* man with *that* tuft of hair", and the matching full facial hair is another key characteristic of the Bagehot look. When the beard arrived, and whether its appearance changed shape and design over the years, is not known.

The facial features most remarked on are his eyes. Described as being 'marvellous' in early childhood; 'large' and 'always noticeable' as a teenager, and 'large', 'dark' and 'brilliant black' when a student, Emilie Barrington provided some further detail of the young adult Walter's dark, round eyes, "his eyelids were thin, and of singularly delicate texture, and the white of the eyeballs was a blue white."

As for the full figure, he was always described as being tall, lissom and lanky, and, as a teenager, "rather thin and long in the legs." In another 1858 love-letter to Eliza, the young banker described himself, in a typically Bagehotian phrase, as being one of the "long awkward currency people."

Recollecting her first sight of Walter, aged 31, in 1857, Emilie Barrington summed him up, "We could not call him handsome, but decidedly he was not plain. He was like no one else. His strong individuality over-rode any classification. He was tall and thin with rather high, narrow square shoulders; his hands were long and delicate and the movements of his fingers very characteristic. He held his fingers quite straight from the knuckles and would often stroke his mouth or rub his forehead when he was thinking or talking."

Some habits and mannerisms

Barrington's last comment neatly leads on to other mannerisms Bagehot was said to have had during his life. For example, she wrote that Walter carried "a very tiny notebook in his waistcoat pocket in which he wrote down ideas as they came to him, resting on a sofa." She also described how, as an adult, he would pace around when he was thinking, and suggesting that not all his ideas reached that notebook, or other written form: "It is exasperating to think of the many good things that came out while he paced up and down the Belgrave Street dining-room, and yet to have made no record of them.

Recalling him years later, she described how he looked when pacing: "He would pace a room when talking, and as the ideas framed themselves in words, he would throw his head back as some animals do when sniffing the air. To us Walter was ever *Walter*, and that meant something quite unlike anybody else."

One habit commented upon by several sources was that of talking aloud to himself when he was, or thought he was, alone. When he wished to relax in afternoons after having worked through the morning, but no horse was available to ride, he would go off on long walks, during which he would speak his thoughts out loud, presumably about his writing or other work.

On that last point, Woodrow Wilson also commented, in an 1898 article: "He liked to talk, indeed, even when there was no one to talk to but himself," recounting (perhaps from his 1896 visit to Langport) that "there are elderly men still to be found at the bank in Langport who remember the overflowing vivacity of the bank's one-time director, and recall how he could oftentimes be overheard talking to himself in his characteristic eager fashion, as he paced all alone up and down the directors' room, in the intervals of business." A more recent biographer, Alastair Buchan, said he was told by an old Langport woman that her father recalled Walter, when riding along the local lanes, "expostulating with himself", and that the workers in the fields "would leave their horses and hide under the hedge to catch what he said."

Mention is often made of his frugality and his dislike of financial speculation, preferring security in money matters – a sensible trait in a banker in those times. In a January 1858 letter to his fiancée, Eliza, when he was telling her that a financial crisis in the City was over, he mused on his preference for periods of financial calm, "I own I like the *sensation* of safety."

As James Grant, his recent financial biographer, put it, "Bagehot saved his money, his friends smiled at his reluctance to spend it." Hutton made the same point, writing that his friend "had the anti-spending instinct in some strength. Generous as Bagehot was - and no one ever hesitated less about giving largely for an adequate end - he always told me, even in boyhood, that spending was disagreeable to him, and that it took something of an effort to pay away money."

One of his favourite anecdotes about his home town of Langport related to its medieval representation in Parliament, and its desire to be relieved of the significant cost of paying their MPs, which he described as "a note of true political sobriety."

Eliza's diaries are littered with examples of Walter missing trains, which she sometimes described as "Walter lost his train." The reason for missing a train is not always explained, though some are weather-related, as on Saturday 17 December 1864, "We expected Walter but the frost & snow made the streets slippery & he missed his train & telegraphed." On Tuesday 13 December 1859, he missed his outbound train so "stayed at home." If it was a return train he either got home well into the evening or nighttime by a later train (the diaries note how frequently he travelled by the last train home), or was forced to stay over and get a train back the following day.

Such mishaps sometimes befell the couple and not just Walter, and it wasn't even their fault, as on Saturday 25 September 1869, when coming back from the Continent. On arrival at Dover, Eliza (and their luggage presumably) was put on the wrong train, and it carried her off to Canterbury while Walter was away dealing with Customs. He had to telegraph ahead to tell the stationmaster at Canterbury to get her off the train, and then he followed by a later train, and they had to stay there overnight.

Langport Station, close to Herd's Hill, which opened in 1853

Worse was when Walter would fall asleep on a train and miss his station, as on Friday 22 September 1876. He was on the last train back from London, fell asleep and "was carried on to Windsor where he supped. He returned hither in a fly, arriving at 1 o'clock am." Walter himself even jokingly blamed Eliza for one such incident in a January 1858 letter, when his new fiancée was in Edinburgh while he was still in Somerset. He was returning to Langport from Bristol and:

> being tired I went to sleep and did not hear them call out the Durston station and was carried on some five and twenty miles to Wellington. There was no train back to Langport so I was obliged to sleep there. It is a wretched little country town, and the best inn had no coffee room and it was fearful to have a fire lighted for me in an unused private room, so I went into the Commercial room and read M. Arnold's tragedy in that congenial spot. I did not mind this - but I did mind having to start at eight the next morning to go home, especially as the sluggish mind of Wellington cd. not be aroused to give me any breakfast. You see this is your fault. If I had not sat up so late, I should not have slept so soundly - I always said you never knew what complications in life were due to the affections. 'There was no end to that sort of thing'. I have undergone Mr. Wylie and the commercial creatures of Wellington for your sake and really you should be grateful.

Walter's hectic commuting and socialising, in London, Somerset and elsewhere, often with early departures and late returns, sometimes worried Eliza. On 11 July 1875 she clearly had a fright about Walter being missing: "Got alarmed at not hearing of Walter, who was due last night, & sent Humphris to town to find out if there had been an accident. ... Emilie stayed with me, ... was lonely & frightened about W." Happily, she noted his return from Langport the very next day and he "came out to dinner."

His chronic ill health did not deter him from risk-taking in his various physical activities, such as riding and hunting. Indeed Emilie Barrington suggested that this aspect was part of his enjoyment of hunting. Mention has been made of his exuberance as a young child, and scaring his mother by running around the unprotected top of the nearby Burton Pynsent monument.

In a November 1857 love-letter, when he is marvelling at how excited he is at being so totally in love, he claimed that it even made him "vault over the sofa with exultation."

Health and ill-health

It is a little ironic that much of the existing information about Bagehot's health comes from his wife Eliza's diaries, whose entries are themselves full of the almost daily recordings of her own maladies. Westwater observed that "life became increasingly populated with dentists and doctors." Walter's frequent illnesses of various types and degrees had significant impacts on the progress of his education and even, in 1868, his potential electoral ambitions, as well as on both his career path and on his work itself.

It was often difficult to separate cause and effect in relation to bouts of ill-health and periods of especially pressured work or home life, as in the period when he took over from James Wilson at *The Economist* from 1859. The regular Christmas trip to Herd's Hill that year was delayed from Christmas Eve to Boxing Day because both he and Eliza were suffering from headaches.

Both he and his father became ill after the death and funeral of his mother, Edith, in the late winter of 1870. Her death had come as a shock, and he only found out about it second-hand while in the capital, being informed by his brother-in-law, Russell Barrington, at Cannon Street Station. Emilie described how "the news had come to him as a staggering blow. He looked scared, my husband said, and his eyes wild. He exclaimed briefly, as if astonished at the sound of his own words – 'My mother is dead'."

He would try to work on through bouts of illness, even seeking assistance, as in the summer of 1869, when Eliza had gone to the Continent to take the waters, and Walter telegrammed Emilie a week later, asking her to come and nurse him. She explained the arrangement they adopted, "I read poetry to him and he dictated his Economist articles to me. They came out with great ease, and though so ill, it seemed no difficulty to him to use his mind."

He seemed to have had a fear of doctors. and would try to avoid having to be treated by them. The diaries recount that in 1866 he accidentally jabbed his umbrella tip into his thumb and refused to visit a doctor until the wound was so badly infected that a doctor had to bleed it. In 1871 he even lanced a swelling on his palate in order to avoid a doctor's visit.

As was common in Victorian times, he suffered issues with his teeth, and the diaries record his trips to dentists, sometimes in graphic detail. It would afflict him even on holiday, as in the autumn of 1867 when he and Eliza were touring the South West. They had to cut short their trip because of his toothache, and Bagehot had to visit a dentist in Bridgwater on the way home.

The diaries note that in the late 1860s both he and Eliza went to two American dentists who were practising in London, Mr Ballard and Dr Coffin. American dentistry was known for advances such as the use of chloroform as an anaesthetic, and Eliza records several instances of having her teeth out under chloroform.

Dr Charles R Coffin, an American dentist working in London, treated the Bagehots

On 11 January 1869, "Walter came home to lunch and remained, being knocked up by the dentist snipping off his two last top teeth". Having disposed of the upper set, matters moved on to the lower teeth, as noted on 7 February 1876, "W had his lower front teeth broken off by Mr Knight."

He had already written indirectly about this in an 1853 essay, "It is only people who have had a tooth out, that really know the dentist's waiting-room. Yet such people, for the time at least, know nothing but that and their tooth.... So, on a greater scale, the man of painful experience knows but too well what has hurt him, and where and why."

During the winter of 1867-68, the extent of his ill-health became clearer when a slight chill developed into a severe internal inflammation, which laid him up for a long period, even, unusually for him, preventing him from reading. During a convalescent trip afterwards, he suffered slight relapses, and he began to rely on assistance with his work from others, such as Robert Giffen at *The Economist*.

While living in Wimbledon in the early 1870s, he had periods when he was forced to stay at home through illness, and took to reading to take his mind off his work. He would send Eliza or Emilie to Smith's library at Wimbledon Station, insisting on 'light' reading and 'easy' novels, "not George Eliot, that was work." Giffen would visit him at home to consult him on matters relating to *The Economist*.

His health deteriorated as he got older, although he was still only in middle age. To take one year as an example, 1875, he is recorded as suffering, amongst other ailments, from two bouts of flu and two colds, as well as rheumatism and neuralgia.

Conversation and wit

An essential part of Bagehot's character was the quality of his conversation, an aspect highlighted and praised by many. To cite two people who knew him in person, Lord Bryce claimed that "One seemed to gain more profit as well as pleasure from a talk with him than with almost anyone else," and his cousin Timothy Smith Osler agreed, "As an instrument for arriving at truth, I never knew anything like a talk with Bagehot." Though these laudatory comments, almost equating him with Oscar Wilde or Samuel Johnson, must be taken with a pinch of salt, it seems clear that, in private conversation especially in social or domestic settings, he was very good company.

Emilie Barrington described Bagehot at Wilson family gatherings in London in the 1860s. "No subject was needed to make a conversation notable, everything was a subject with Walter Bagehot. The discussion of serious matters, equally with those of a frivolous kind, was of no less original a quality. Everything he said carried with it that profound sense of reality which was so strong a characteristic of his mind." She recorded similar sentiments regarding Bagehot family gatherings in Langport.

His friend Richard Hutton quoted a woman friend of Bagehot's as saying that she never asked him a question "without his answer making you either think or laugh, or both think and laugh together." He did not dominate or hog conversation but would be happy to participate in general discussion along with one or more other participants. He could, however, be sardonic and even cutting when he deemed it necessary. This ease contrasted with his poor showings as a public speaker, especially at election campaigns.

As came through also in his writings, he was naturally witty and could reel off an epigram or anecdote with ease. Gladstone's daughter, Helen, recounted a remark of his at one of the great man's famous Thursday breakfasts, that he knew what a nut felt like when it was going to be cracked, as he once got his head caught between a cart-shed and a lamp-post. Near the end of his life, when he was breakfasting with his young nephew, Guy Barrington, and the boy could not open his egg, he told him, "Go on, Guy, Hit it hard on the head. It has no friends."

Walter was self-deprecating about these characteristics, as in a letter on 4 January 1858 to Eliza, "I assure you I still like to talk theology very much when I am started, but I am lazy and quiescent in all intellectual conversation. I like talking and do talk a great deal somehow, still I require a stimulus - a nudge in my elegant native dialect from without, or I do not begin."

Bagehot described the 1851 Great Exhibition as 'a great fair under a cucumber frame'

PART TWO

HIS WRITINGS

CHAPTER THIRTEEN

Bagehot the writer

This, and the following two chapters, look at Bagehot's body of written work, upon which his reputation largely rests. No attempt is made to provide a detailed description or analysis of what he wrote. Rather they seek to examine how, why and to what extent they provide the basis of that reputation, in terms of his writing in general, and in relation to the two particular areas where his fame is greatest and enduring, banking and finance, and government and politics.

Matters biographical, historical and literary

Throughout his life, Bagehot found time to write on subjects that were not primarily related to current affairs. These were mainly essays on literary subjects – especially novels and poetry – and on people or events from history, such as William Pitt, Bolingbroke and the Great Reform Act, as well as historians like Macauley and Gibbon. He was not writing as an academic literary critic or historian, any more than he was a professional political scientist or economist. He was more an example of the Victorian amateur polymath.

In these areas, he appeared to write about people or subjects that interested him, whether that interest was long-standing or transitory. These can be distinguished from his political profiles of contemporary major players, which form part of his day-to-day journalism. His essay on 'Lord Althorp and the Reform Act of 1832', which appeared in the November 1876 *Fortnightly Review*, was the last piece published in a journal other than *The Economist* in his lifetime.

Adam Smith and William Shakespeare – the subjects of two of Bagehot's most famous essays

His technique of approaching particular issues or events through a biographical lens – made obvious in the titles of some of them, such as 'Shakespeare - the individual' (sometimes entitled 'Shakespeare – the man'), and 'Adam Smith as a person' - did not commend his work to some critics, who saw it as a way of avoiding matters which either did not interest him or were beyond his capabilities. Nevertheless, he found it a convenient and helpful approach, and was happy to defend it, as in his 1852 Hartley Coleridge essay "'We have described Hartley's life at length for a peculiar reason. It is necessary to comprehend his character to appreciate his works; and there is no way of delineating character but by a selection of characteristic sayings and actions."

A significant proportion of his output, especially in his earlier years, dealt with literary subjects, though he did not cover areas such as art or music (until very late in life, he was known for his dislike of music). His first published work in 1847, when he was only 21, was a review of a long poem, *Festus*, then in vogue, and poetry was a passion all his life. Poetry was, for him, a serious and profound subject, not mere entertainment. He wrote on poets such as Shelley, Wordsworth, Tennyson, Coleridge, Milton, Shakespeare, Cowper, Browning, the Frenchman, Pierre-Jean de Béranger, as well as his friend, Arthur Hugh Clough. He also wrote about novelists such as Dickens, Scott, Sterne and Thackeray, and the lesser-known Emily Eden, author of the 1859 *The Semi-Detached House*. Though he was an acquaintance of George Eliot – whom he publicly described as 'the greatest living writer of fiction' - and of Anthony Trollope, he did not dedicate an article to either.

His friend, the poet Arthur Clough, and his favourite author, Sir Walter Scott

It was with his literary output that Bagehot came under especially heavy criticism for not being a 'real' critic, in the sense of applying existing or new theories to the literary works he was examining, and for being pleasant but superficial. Bagehot would probably have accepted the particular charge of not being an academic literary critic and not have regarded it as a failing.

William Haley, who wrote the introduction to Bagehot's literary essays in the Stevas *Collected Works*, suggested that:

> Bagehot's approach to literature is rarely literary. As a critic, Bagehot evolved no theory that stands up to examination, inaugurated no fashion, made no discoveries, rearranged no order of values, founded no school. The literary quibbles that have long, and to an increasing degree, delighted the academic critics, he ignored. He was very often more interested in the man he was dealing with than in his writings. He used the works as signposts to the author's character, and he sought broadly to place both in a setting of the practice of life.

His early death at the age of 51 raises the obvious question of what would Bagehot the writer have done had he lived. Would he have completed his unfinished book on political economy (examined in a later chapter)? Would have he adopted the template of *Physics and Politics* (see below) to examine other more novel areas of interest, or areas he had tackled much earlier in his life, before *The Economist* consumed so much of his life after 1860? Biographers and colleagues, believing that he was still mentally sound, and even at the height of his powers, have suggested he would have done something along these lines. Emilie Barrington thought that he would have returned to areas like poetry and religion that in later life he could only indulge in his spare time, such as through his membership of the Metaphysical Society. Robert Giffen had suggested that he may well have focussed on a history of political ideas or "some other work of general philosophy." In practice, such speculation is fruitless, as it would depend on the state of his health; the length and intensity of his involvement with *The Economist* and in his banking and other business activities, and any desire to seek pastures new, such as further attempts to become an MP.

Aspects of his style and technique

Like all published writers, he wanted his works to have an impact. As he put it himself in a November 1857 letter to his future wife, "I am afraid I covet *'power'* influence over people's wills faculties and conduct more in proportion than I can quite defend. I think this a very good thing too in many ways, but I do not quite approve the intensity w th which I feel it. Until I knew you it was certainly the strongest feeling I had ever known..."

At the core of Bagehot's writing was a desire to be understood, so his style was intentionally accessible and clear for his era. It was even described by some admirers as conversational. From a 21st century perspective, though, many of his pieces, especially his long-form essays and the chapters of his books, may seem very wordy, full of complex sentences and phrases and, at times, almost rambling.

He must be judged alongside the style of his period, where such verbosity was the norm, especially for the literary journals that he regularly wrote for, then at or near their zenith during Bagehot's time. This is partly a result of the inevitable skewing resulting from it being mainly his longer pieces that endure and against which he has been judged. His shorter pieces, especially if they are news or analysis on current events, largely in *The Economist*, would not have been intended for posterity and generally do not appear in collections of h s work.

Use of what may be described as digression, humour, paradox, epigrams – the quality of many of which makes him so quotable to this day - and similar devices would be available to him in the luxury of the long-form essay. He intentionally used them to illuminate, not to obfuscate. Clarity was an essential aim. In his 1852 essay on the poet and literary figure, Hartley Coleridge (son of the more famous Samuel Taylor Coleridge), he explained:

> We believe that the knack in style is to write like a human being. Some think they must be wise, some elaborate, some concise ... But legibility is given to those who neglect these notions, and are willing to be themselves, to write their own thoughts in their own words, in the simplest words, in the words wherein they were thought ...

One recent close student of his work, Martha Westwater, even suggested that "Bagehot could and did write clever nonsense that drew the reader into a friendly intimacy."

He often adopted surprising stances, praising unlikely characteristics, not just moderation, but even stupidity and dullness, as well as the acceptance of 'error', in public life, which helped to make his arguments more eye-catching. His senior colleague at *The Economist*, Robert Giffen, referring to Bagehot's style in his maturer years, wrote that he aimed "to be conversational, to put things in the most direct and picturesque manner, as people would talk to each other in common speech, to remember and use expressive colloquialisms. Such Americanisms as the 'shrinkage' of values he had a real liking for, and constantly applied them."

Giffen thought that this informality of style was clearly seen in his financial writings, much being aimed directly at the very people in 'the City' he was writing about, especially when he was in prescriptive rather than purely descriptive mode:

> He had always some typical City man in his mind's eye; a man not skilled in literature or the turnings of phrases, with a limited vocabulary and knowledge of theory, but keen as to facts, and reading for the sake of information and guidance respecting what vitally concerned him. To please this ideal City man, Bagehot would use harsh and crude or redundant expressions, sometimes ungrammatical if tried by ordinary tests; anything to drive his meaning home.

A good example of Bagehot (when only 26) in full flow on financial matters comes from an 1852 *Inquirer* article, 'Investments':

> People won't take 2 per cent; they won't bear a loss of income. Instead of that dreadful event, they invest their careful savings in something impossible - a canal to Kamchatka, a railway to Watchet, a plan for animating the Dead Sea, a corporation for shipping skates to the Torrid Zone. A century or two ago, the Dutch burgomasters, of all people in the world, invented the most imaginative occupation. They speculated in *impossible tulips*. It was quite understood that they were impossible: nobody had ever seen such species as were sold, nobody ever wished to see such species as were bought; but money was plenty. There had been originally a 'legitimate demand' for gardening-roots and soothing flowers; and out of that the whole grew.

How he obtained the material he needed for his written work is instructive. His own personal experience as a professional banker and man of business obviously informed his writings, both of the journalist and essayist kind. He has been regularly and heavily criticised by professionals and academics since his death for being an untrained amateur merely dabbling in many of the more specialised and scientific areas he tackled, or even in the more esoteric and technical aspects of the areas that he did have a working knowledge of. He was accused of adopting some of his signature techniques largely to mask his inadequacies for more profound thought, rather than attempting the hard work of study of all the available literature, original thought and empirical research. Bagehot would, doubtless, accept these criticisms on their face but respond that he never pretended that he was aiming to be an academic theorist, or a professional scientist.

As a writer, and an editor of a respected publication, he would mix in that society, not just because he gradually became part of it, mainly through his marriage to the Wilson family, but because it, rather than text-book or archival research, was the primary source of information for his writings, and for the news and information that underlay them. As his recent biographer, James Grant, neatly put it, "to this end he traipsed from office to office, and informant to informant."

He accepted the practical necessity of this 'insider' role, as he admitted to his sister-in-law Zoë Wilson in a letter of early January 1860: "The great change of late to me is that having the Economist to look after I come to London and call on public characters and sit (like Jet [Emilie Wilson's dog]) with my mouth open hearing what they say."

The 'bad' writer

Many commentators, including many admirers, have marvelled at how a writer and editor of Bagehot's status and skills could have so many faults in the actual process of writing, from grammar and spelling to inaccuracies of quotations and facts, or that a practical banker and man of business could be so careless at basic arithmetical skills.

This went back to his youthful years. His sister-in-law Emilie Barrington described a letter of May 1845 by the 19-year-old Walter as "writing carelessly, his spelling was often erratic." He was chided for this by both his parents, especially his mother. When she had difficulty understanding one of her son's letters around that same time, she did not spare the sarcasm in her reply: "till Bagehot's grammar and dictionary supersede the old ones, we must spell and divide not according to sound, but the common usage of the schools."

Editing Bagehot's letters for his *Collected Works*, Stevas explained how he dealt with these issues:

> Texts transcribed from manuscript follow the original almost exactly, reproducing Bagehot's spelling, punctuation and capitalization. Mis-spellings, frequent in Bagehot's schoolboy letters, are indicated in a footnote only when likely to mislead or puzzle the reader; omission or misplacing of the apostrophe has been reproduced without a footnote...

Even his closest friend and college, Richard Holt Hutton, in his *Memoir* of Bagehot, did not avoid dealing with his stylistic failings:

> He was always absentminded about minutiae. For instance, to the last, he could not correct a proof well, and was sure to leave a number of small inaccuracies, harshnesses, and slipshodnesses in style, uncorrected. He declared at one time that he was wholly unable to 'add up,' and in his mathematical exercises in college he had habitually been inaccurate in trifles. ... This habitual difficulty - due, I believe, to a preoccupied imagination - in attending to small details, made a banker's duties seem irksome and formidable to him at first; and even to the last, in his most effective financial papers, he would generally get some one else to look after the precise figures for him.

His close colleague at *The Economist* in Bagehot's latter years, Robert Giffen, himself a noted statistician, was a little more indulgent of his boss's numerical lapses:

> From the manipulation of figures he was most averse, and he rather boasted that he was unable to add up. But he was a most excellent mathematician, and no one could be so careful, as he was about the logic of the figures got together for his articles, which he always most carefully scrutinized. He would frequently point out that his figures were illustrative merely, and did not by themselves establish an argument.

Without doubt, the most heartfelt and frustrated critic in this respect was Forrest Morgan, the editor of the 1889 five-volume collection of Bagehot's works by the Travelers Insurance Company of Hartford, Connecticut. In his preface he wrote that the compilation was meant to be a simple exercise, without any significant substantive editing. However he soon found that major editing, lasting several years, was an "extreme necessity" due to, for example, "the discovery that Bagehot's own matter was in almost as corrupt a state as his extracts from other writers." He listed examples of the "shocking state of Bagehot ... there is nothing even approaching it in the case of any other English writer of high rank since Shakespeare's time." He blamed much of it on Bagehot himself for not doing even the minimum remedial work on his own proofs, accusing him of "evidently never even looked at most of them at all. These slips cover almost the entire possible range of human blunders, and are sometimes of serious moment."

He carried on for several more paragraphs in similar vein, best illustrated by the memorable remarks of Bagehot's most recent biographer, James Grant, encompassing Morgan's *cri de coeur* with his own, slightly unfair, take on Bagehot's shortcomings:

> Morgan wanted the readers to know – he really wanted them to know, as he had spent years of toil – that within the first rank of English authors, Bagehot was the all-time, hands-down worst speller, fact-checker (he did not actually check facts), quotation-verifier (he made them up), and proofreader (he didn't even bother).

Writing on holiday

One habit Bagehot had was writing while ostensibly on holiday, particularly if he was working on something substantial, where he had time and space to focus without distractions, especially in his later years when heavily engaged with *The Economist*.

In December 1856, he had written to his great friend, Hutton, scorning the very idea of a real holiday, doing nothing substantial, as merely time-wasting: "As to holidays, it is one of the lessons of life to learn to be independent of them. They are scarcely to be obtained by people in regular employment except in very fortunate circumstances. I have some right to say this myself for except when I was at Roscoe's last autumn, I have not been a week without doing *some* business."

He reinforced that view in a September 1862 letter: "It moves my bitter envy to hear of a man's daring to go to a country where the post is such as you describe. My best idea of a holiday is half a dozen letters daily."

Whether or not that remained his view in his maturer years, married and with a full and high-pressured professional career, it is certainly noteworthy how often he and Eliza (who had been used to continental trips in her pre-Walter years) went away on holidays within Britain and in Europe. Many, if not most of these holidays entailed touring around, rarely staying at the one place for more than a few days, which, in those times, must have consumed a fair proportion of their supposed breaks. As Emilie Barrington memorably noted, he "carried his mind with him during his holidays, and few of his travels were planned without their being linked to some interest, literary, historical or political."

Eliza's diaries and Emilie Barrington's biography are full of examples of his holiday writing habit. For example, in May 1862, the Bagehots went for a short break to Bognor, to enable him to write the pamphlet, *Count your Enemies and Economise your Expenditure*. During their autumn 1866 tour of the South West, he finished & sent off his chapter on 'Changes of Ministry' in his English Constitution series for the *Fortnightly Review*. Three years later, and despite illness during a continental tour he wrote a short article on the money market for *The Economist*. In 1875, when he was struggling with his ambitious book on economics, he did much of his writing during 'holidays' around Southern England. The following extracts from Eliza's 1868 diary entry provide a typical flavour of this:

> We left Langport 3 for Lyme Regis, stopped at Axminster for tea and to write letters, sending off revise of second number Physics and Politics for Fortnightly Review. Reached Lyme Regis at 7. 27th March. We drove to Axminster before lunch to send the Money Article for Economist.

Physics and Politics

Traditionally, the three books that are regarded as cementing Bagehot's reputation are *The English Constitution*, *Lombard Street* and *Physics and Politics*. The first two will be covered in the succeeding chapters dealing with their respective subject areas, so it is convenient to consider *Physics and Politics* here, as it is, in many respects, an outlier.

It was, like *The English Constitution*, largely the product of a number of already-published essays, though these five essays were published over a span of over four years (late 1967 to early 1872) - largely due to Bagehot's ill-health – plus a new concluding chapter for the book published in December 1872. This all detracted from the overall work having a satisfactory cohesiveness, as Bagehot himself recognised at the start of the last chapter, "[T]here is a risk of tedious repetition, but on a subject both obscure and important, any defect is better than an appearance of vagueness."

Its very title attracts attention and perhaps puzzlement. In Bagehot's time, 'physics' did not have the specialised meaning it has now, but was more akin to a synonym for science in general. 'Politics' referred not to partisan politics, but to the more general organisation and operation of political societies. Even so, critics of the book over the last century or more have suggested alternative more accurate titles, such as 'Biology and Politics', 'Biology and Sociology' or 'Biological Interpretation of History.'

Bagehot's subtitle, *Thoughts on the application of the principles of 'Natural Selection' and 'Inheritance' to political society,* not only gives a clearer idea of his intended subject matter, it also signposts the problems that the book would have for more modern readers. It can be treated – or dismissed – as an example of 19th century Social Darwinism, dealing with the ranking of various 'races' in terms of intellect and civilisation, through Darwinian natural selection and evolution. Though generally regarded as acceptable in its time, the calamitous impact of such theories in the 20th century have inevitably made them 'beyond the pale'. So too any book or writer thought to be propounding them. It makes it difficult to examine Bagehot's book without considering this hugely negative perspective.

However a partial defence could be made to these accusations. While the assumptions inherent in it do reek of Western, European superiority, its language is not so explicit. There are relatively few uses of words like, 'superior/inferior' or 'white/black, though 'savage' is common throughout. More common is the notion of 'civilisation', suggesting that Bagehot is concerned more with that than 'race' per se. It is intended to be a study of the evolution of civilised society or societies, rather than of particular 'races'. 'Civilisation' is measured by the rather optimistic notion of development from an age of conflict to what he called an 'age of discussion'. Read this way, its potential toxicity may be, to a marginal degree, diluted.

If such criticism was based on a work being 'of its own time', but now no longer valid in more enlightened times, that is one thing, but *Physics and Politics* has also been criticised as not being a great work even for the latter 19th century. He was profoundly interested in then-current theories in areas such as law, science, ethnology and psychology that were revolutionising 19th century thinking, and some of which he had encountered through both his formal education and through connections, (both family and friends), to leading thinkers in such fields. He was trying to apply them to his more familiar arena of government and politics, by writing, in effect, the 'scientific' companion to works like *The English Constitution*.

Because of the 'historical' subject matter, his approach is much more speculative than descriptive, trying to provide a plausible narrative of the millennia-long story of the development of human civilisation, applying these various strands of contemporary thought. Ambitious stuff, indeed. And it provided the main thrust of modern criticism – even dismissal – of the book.

He was accused of not basing his ideas on his own research or original theorising, but by unscientifically cherry-picking from current popular thinking to make his hotch-potch argument superficially coherent and sound. These ideas included Sir Henry Maine's legal idea of a development of a society based on 'status' to one based on 'contract'; Darwinism in its narrow senses of evolution and natural selection, and wider 'Social Darwinism' such as the 'survival of the fittest' and struggles for limited resources ideas of Herbert Spencer and Thomas Malthus.

James Grant summed up this critical approach most compellingly, describing *Physics and Politics* as:

> a production not of science, but of supposition and imagination. It is anthropology without the fieldwork, science without the laboratory, and scholarship without the footnotes. It is the daring and ambitious speculation of an educated Victorian amateur on a branch of knowledge about which he admits he knows little. ... Today, its merit lies less in what Bagehot said than in the zestful way he said it.

CHAPTER FOURTEEN
Government, politics and the constitution

Bagehot's enduring reputation is based in part on his writing on government, politics and the constitution. As with his other writings, on banking and finance, Bagehot's output can be divided into two broad categories, albeit with some degree of overlap.

The first was his regular journalistic output. He was, especially during his long tenure at *The Economist*, a political columnist. He was largely reacting to, and analysing, issues of the moment, be they legislation in Parliament; crises within governments and parties; elections, or political events in the wider world. It would be unfair to decry such writing in a weekly newspaper or magazine as 'tomorrow's fish-and-chip paper', but this context of 'immediacy' is crucial to the understanding of much of his output.

An important part of this contemporary political writing, as it remains to this day, was the production of profiles of the major politicians of the day, such as Gladstone and Disraeli. Bagehot was very clear that, however intrusive this may seem to the subjects being written about – especially if they were, like Gladstone, close professional or personal acquaintances – there was a clear public interest in this type of article. As he wrote in his major and controversial *National Review* essay on Gladstone in 1860:

> We believe that Quarterly essayists have a peculiar mission in relation to the characters of public men. We believe it is their duty to be personal. ... Public men must bear this criticism as they can. Those whose names are perpetually in men's mouths must not be pained if singular things are sometimes said of them. Still some deliberate truth should be spoken of our statesmen; and if Quarterly essayists do not speak it, who will? We fear it will remain unspoken.

In the second category stand his more considered, thoughtful works, be they essays in various journals, such as *The Economist*, or in published books or pamphlets. By their nature, such works are, or are intended to be, more enduring, and in the context of this chapter, their pinnacle is his 1867 masterpiece, *The English Constitution*, itself a collection of previously published lengthy articles.

It would be too simplistic to say that the former, more immediate writings endure largely through their readability rather than by their analysis, as a repository of quotable phrases rather than original insights, and that it is with the second category that his reputation rests. Matters are more complex than that - timeless quotes abound in the books and longer essays, and much of the lengthy analyses of the longer form have become redundant and forgotten.

The main point here, from the perspective of enduring fame or celebrity, and to what extent he is deserving of such, is that his work has to be taken in its proper context. To describe him as a man of his time is a truism, whether used critically or otherwise, but one that is often misused by admirers and critics alike.

Allied to this is the underlying question of whether he was *describing* ('what is') or *prescribing* ('what should be') and the extent to which he can be praised or criticised for either. For example, to complain that it doesn't accurately describe the current 21st

107

century constitution, or that his prescriptions don't apply to it, is rather meaningless, especially for someone who dealt more with practice than theory.

For Bagehot, a key purpose of writing *The English Constitution* was to correct what he saw as the accepted, but, in his view, idealised and misleading, descriptions of this country's constitution and politics, especially in the vital operative inter-relationships between its core institutions such as Parliament, Government and Monarchy. It did not follow that he would necessarily approve of, or champion, every aspect of what he found. His description of the constitution was just as likely as to be potentially improvable in many respects, both for its own time, and inevitably for the changing circumstances of the future. In practice, his work contained a mixture of description of what he had found; comment on whether or not he approved of what he had described, and whether, and how, it could or should be improved upon.

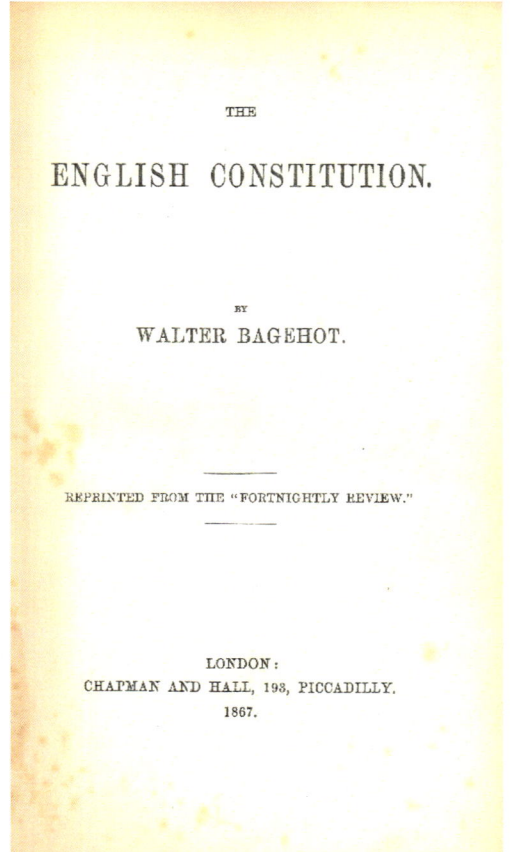

First edition of The English constitution, 1867

What he wrote about

To say that Bagehot is an authority on the constitution, or government or politics is not to suggest that he comprehensively covered all these topics. Though his university study and legal training would allow him some intellectual perspective, he was not an academic, whether a constitutional lawyer or political scientist, nor did he aspire to be. His accessible style should be seen as complementing the contemporary and later classics of constitutional law and political science.

He did not focus on many areas that we would now regard as being squarely within these fields, such as public administration, human and civil rights, local government or even the constitutional role of the judiciary. His arena was that of the major institutions of the Executive – the political Government and the Monarchy – and the Legislative – the two houses of Parliament, their members, parties and elections – and this was examined largely through a metropolitan prism, confined to Westminster and Whitehall (and its related clubland and elite society, and The City, where relevant). Wider Britsh or foreign affairs were generally approached as to how and why they affected that close-knit class-based polity.

As his status and reputation grew, he became part of that society. He wrote based on what he saw and what he was told as a trusted and respected insider. He recognised and relished this privileged status: "Living really in the political world is the greatest possible gain in a political country; knowing at first hand what others know at second hand only. The characters and the play of political life are not otherwise accessible." That would inevitably skew his focus and narrow his perspectives. Yet it is by being this 'insider' that his views and insights can be valued. He was someone who knew what he was writing about.

Uncovering the secrets

A significant part of the influence of Bagehot lies in how he set about analysing the British constitution in his own unique way. He examined what he saw as the reality of the 'living' system that operated all around him, rather than what was handed down in the theoretical, textbook 'idealised' constitution – especially 18th century 'separation of powers' orthodoxies ie the separation of the Executive, Legislative and Judicial branches of government. From this analysis, he derived what he regarded as the true secret of that 'real' British constitution, the discovery of which would sweep away all the deliberate and accidental concealments that had hidden its essential truths.

There are two main aspects of his 'discovery' of the secret of the core mid-Victorian constitution. First there is the distinction between the *dignified* and the *efficient* parts of the constitution, and second the claim that the *efficient secret* of the constitution was the fusion, by way of the Cabinet, of the executive and legislative functions of government.

This classification, much like the results of empirical research in a scientific context, helped set the parameters of future discussion. Many writers from Bagehot's time onwards in effect saw their task of interpreting the constitution as one of allocating or reallocating various bits of the constitutional jigsaw into these Bagehotian 'dignified' and 'efficient' compartments, and through this process to discover the new `efficient secret', or the new one true source of political power, if it had changed. This can be seen most obviously since the 1960s with the claimed replacement of 'Cabinet government' by 'Prime Ministerial government'.

To some extent, Bagehot's analysis was not so revolutionary. He deliberately oversimplified what he claimed were the standard orthodoxies in his time, especially the 'separation of powers' between Government and Parliament, so as to emphasise the novelty of his particular approach. Bagehot's fame and value lie not so much in the originality of his thesis but the fact that, with his journalistic skills, he could put it into memorable form; he gave definitive form to what became the new orthodoxy.

This division of the components of the constitution into dignified and efficient elements was central, as it showed not only how power was actually located and allocated, but also provided the glue and mystique essential to make it operate effectively. He defined the dignified parts as "those which excite and preserve the reverence of the population" and the efficient parts as "those by which [the constitution] in fact works and rules." The dignified elements are preserved in order to conceal how government is run and how, and by whom, decisions are actually made, and so to ensure allegiance to the efficient parts.

Central to this analysis was the discovery of the 'efficient secret'. Bagehot claimed that "it may be defined as the close union, the nearly complete fusion, of the executive and legislative powers ... The connecting link is the Cabinet. ... A Cabinet is a combining committee - a hyphen which joins, a buckle which fastens, the legislative part of the State to the executive part of the State. In its origin it belongs to the one, in its functions it belongs to the other." In other words, what he was claiming was that, far from there being a separation between the Legislature (Parliament) and the Executive (Government), these two core branches of the political system were virtually combined as one, and this was achieved by means of the Cabinet. The Cabinet comprised members of the two Houses of Parliament, but operated as the 'board of directors' of the Government.

Whether or not one accepts this analysis – it seems strange now to think of the Cabinet as being any sort of parliamentary committee – this notion neatly encapsulates two central aspects of the British system. First, that Ministers operate within and through Parliament, and, secondly, that the Government was no longer in practice merely a loose collection of the Monarch's appointed ministers (with the Prime Minister as its head), but a collective and autonomous entity, linked to the Monarch nominally, but in practice bound to the Prime Minister, and exercising its mandate through its majority in Parliament.

With this approach, Bagehot could examine the major components – the Government of Ministers and Prime Minister, the two Houses of Parliament, and the Monarchy (the Judicial arm is notably absent from much of this core analysis) – and their power and practical relationships with each other, in some detail.

Constitutional monarchy

A closer look at one of the key components of Bagehot's constitutional system will suffice to demonstrate his views, style and influence. Perhaps the best example of this is his analysis of the monarchy, which came to be largely accepted as the template for British constitutional monarchy in the modern, democratic age.

By the mid-19th century, the monarchy had transitioned from the efficient to the dignified side of the constitution. Yet it probably became the most important such element, as Bagehot asserted at the outset of his analysis: "The use of the Queen in a dignified capacity is incalculable. Without her in England, the present English Government would fail and pass away." As Bagehot observed, it is a relatively intelligible form of government for the public. Even better, because it involves a royal family as well as much pomp and circumstance, it is what we would describe nowadays as a fascinating never-ending soap opera, of marriages (and divorces) and other domestic episodes which humanise the institution:

A *family* on the throne is an interesting idea also. It brings down the pride of sovereignty to the level of petty life. No feeling could seem more childish than the enthusiasm of the English at the marriage of the Prince of Wales. They treated as a great political event, what, looked at as a matter of pure business, was very small indeed. ... A princely marriage is the brilliant edition of a universal fact, and as such, it rivets mankind. ... Just so a royal family sweetens politics by the seasonable addition of nice and pretty events. It introduces irrelevant facts into the business of government, but they are facts which speak to 'men's bosoms' and employ their thoughts. To state the matter shortly, royalty is a government in which the attention of the nation is concentrated on one person doing interesting actions.

Bagehot was mainly writing at a time when Queen Victoria had retreated from public life after the death of Prince Albert in 1861, and the monarchy's popularity was vulnerable. He recognised that "a retired widow and an unemployed youth" (i.e. the Prince of Wales) were objects of fascination to the outside world, but they had to put on a suitably impressive show to maintain that interest.

There is a delicate balance here, because this normalisation has to be kept within strict bounds behind a wall of secrecy, so as to maintain the necessary degree of reverence, and thereby its effectiveness. Bagehot famously recognised, "if you begin to poke about it you cannot reverence it. ... Its mystery is its life. We must not let in daylight upon magic. We must not bring the Queen into the combat of politics, or she will cease to be reverenced by all combatants; she will become one combatant among many." Recent decades have demonstrated the grave risks of drawing the monarch into the actual governing of the country, and partisan politics, over issues like the appointment and removal of Prime Ministers, to the possible refusal of assent to legislation, or to the prorogation of Parliament.

If the monarchy – or in its more abstract legal sense, the Crown – properly fulfils its 'dignified' role and function, it provides the necessary cloak of authority and legitimacy which allows the actual Government to govern in its name.

George V and George VI were taught Bagehot's views

A constitutional monarch however is, in Bagehot's view, more than a mere cypher. He or she had a genuine if limited role in government, especially through her ministers and Prime Minister. Bagehot characterised this as three limited but essential rights - 'the right to be consulted, the right to encourage, and the right to warn'. He himself warned that "a king of great sense and sagacity would want no others. He would find that his having no others would enable him to use these with singular effect." Had he lived into the present day, he would certainly have regarded Elizabeth II's reign as a good example of this high constitutional role.

Whether or not Bagehot was being descriptive or prescriptive (or both) in his study of the British monarchy, the following decades showed that his analysis was not just held in high regard, it was the one that was taught to heirs to the throne as to how to be a good constitutional monarch. The future George V received such an education from a Cambridge scholar in Bagehot's *The English Constitution*, as the Royal Archives attest, which stood him in good stead during the extreme constitutional crisis over Irish Home Rule in 1913. The future George VI also studied Bagehot at Cambridge, and the then Princess Elizabeth was also schooled in Bagehot before and during the Second World War, as was famously fictionalised recently in an episode of the popular Netflix series, *The Crown*. There is no reason to believe that this has not continued with the then Prince Charles and with Prince William.

The enduring Bagehot

The risk with any orthodoxy is that it itself becomes stale or outdated, vulnerable to challenge. The mid-Victorian constitution is very different from that of the 21st century, mirroring the vast changes in society and world politics. The very democratisation of politics that Bagehot was witnessing with some trepidation, and which, through his 'system' he sought to manage and control, has transformed this country. Bagehot was in no modern sense a democrat. To him, the universal franchise and all that might flow from it risked undermining the very system he was describing. One of his greatest admirers, the early 20th century US President, Woodrow Wilson, described this 'deeper lack' in Bagehot: "He has no sympathy with the voiceless body of the people, with the 'mass of unknown men'. He conceives the work of government to be a work which is possible only to the instructed few."

Bagehot's classifications provided a method of discovering constitutional changes over time by reallocating various components between the 'dignified' and 'efficient'. It became the default description. A political scientist put it rather neatly in a 1975 essay: "since Bagehot's death in 1877, the British political world still speaks, writes and teaches in Bagehot's terms. ... We were still bounded by the classic British parliamentary system for which Bagehot is the best interpreter."

A 2017 BBC Radio4 programme commemorating the 150th anniversary of the publication of *The English Constitution* was entitled, 'What would Bagehot say?' Indeed.

CHAPTER FIFTEEN

Banking and finance

Especially in the areas of banking and finance, Bagehot's writings flowed to a large degree from his own practical experience as a country banker, and more widely as a man of business. He took part in his family's extensive mercantile activities in the West Country and in the management of *The Economist* and the *National Review*.

He was writing about finance from a remarkably early age. Two of his first three published articles, while he was still a graduate student of 22 in London in 1848, covered 'the currency monopoly' and a review of J S Mill's *Principles of Political Economy*. He wrote few other such articles until the mid-1850s, when he had settled back into life in Langport as a country banker, but then his desire to write on financial matters grew, and he was published mainly in the *Saturday Review*, and the *National Review*, the latter a journal in which he was heavily involved.

His critical breakthrough in writing for *The Economist* in 1857-8 has already been discussed, and it was based on a series of 12 short articles, under the pseudonym, 'A Banker.' As his responsibilities there developed quickly, his output, both directly in his own articles, and the general supervision and editorship of the magazine's content, became ever more focussed on banking, financial and economic matters.

As with all his writings, his financial output reflects his practical rather than any theoretical, academic focus, which lead some to regard him as a shallow amateur. Hutton, in his 1877 *Memoir* of Bagehot saw this more as a plus rather than a failing. "[E]ven as an economist, Bagehot's most original writing was due less to his deductions from the fundamental axioms of the modern science, than to that deep insight into men which he had gained in many different fields." Thus, the two 1876 *Fortnightly Review* essays on the postulates of political economy "furnish quite an original study in social history and in human nature" and his classic book, *Lombard Street*, "is quite as much a study of bankers and bill-brokers as of the principles of banking."

What marked him out in these fields, Hutton believed, was his unique perspective, because he was fortunate to have qualities which most professional or academic economists and politicians lacked. "What he brought to political and economical science he brought in some sense from outside their normal range, that the man of business and the financier in him fell within such sharp and well-defined limits that he knew better than most of his class where their special weakness lay, and where their special functions ended."

It was this originality of approach that made much of his best work so compelling. The financial journalist, Robert Peston, wrote in 2008 that Bagehot "in the 1870s taught us more-or-less all we know about how to deal with banking panics." While that may well be a touch hyperbolic, it does indicate how, a century and a half after his death, his reputation in the financial arena endures.

Even in the arcane byways of financial and economic matters, his style was refreshingly accessible and direct, while being insightful and shrewd. A recent admirer, the

American financial journalist, James Grant, rated him thus in his 2019 biography: "His eminence was the near-literature of high journalism. Financial journalism is not so high, nor success, when achieved, so lofty. In that quotidian branch of the writing business, Bagehot was a superior commentator though a middling seer..."

As befits a writer and editor of a weekly news magazine, much of his overall financial output was focussed on matters of immediate moment, most of which is now of largely historical interest. The same can be said of his forays into the more esoteric areas such as the role of gold and silver in currency, and the nature of money itself. Nevertheless, he did write many more considered essays, especially on the money markets and central banking, and it is on these, and one book in particular, *Lombard Street*, that his financial reputation rests.

Lombard Street

Just as *The English Constitution* was the most enduring and influential of Bagehot's constitutional writings, so *Lombard Street: a description of the money market* (1873) is similarly the most respected of his writings on banking and finance.

LOMBARD STREET IN 1850, BY T. C. DIBDEN

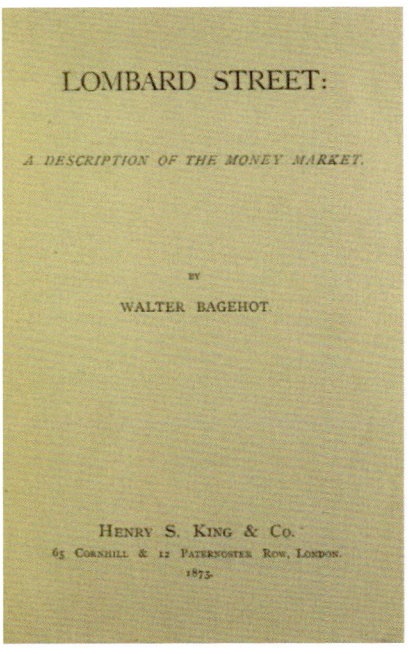

Its initial publication was accompanied by an almost apologetic note from its author. Bagehot described it as a "little book", much delayed – having begun in autumn 1870 – by other commitments and by illness. He feared an unfavourable reception to it, especially from those it mainly concerned, such as the Bank of England, other joint stock banks, private bankers and bill brokers, but defended his views as "they have been slowly matured in Lombard Street itself and ... I may at least ask for the credit of having been impartial in my criticism."

His text began with an explanation of its title, to show that he meant to deal with 'concrete realities,' and to demonstrate that the money market, contrary to conventional wisdom, can be described in plain words. Not for nothing was its sub-title 'a description of the money market'. Not only did it clearly limit the scope of the book –

the money market is only a part, albeit a key one, of the overall financial and economic system – but it was a description of it, and of its key players. Therefore these descriptions play much the same role in this book as his biographical studies play in his wider writings, illuminating the particular area under consideration.

Robert Giffen, his erstwhile colleague at *The Economist* and later a noted public statistician, thought that *Lombard Street* "shows the high-water mark of what Bagehot could do in point of form and execution," describing "its special excellence as a descriptive book,", as well as a valuable contribution to economics. A descriptive approach is of little value if the style of the work is not accessible and readable. As Grant neatly puts it, "*Lombard Street* is a grand tour of living finance under the classical gold standard. ... [It] scintillates."

At the outset, Bagehot uses this unique style to set out what he sees as the ABCs of finance and credit. The start of his first substantive chapter began by adopting David Ricardo's definition of a banker as one who uses other people's money. People who use their own money are merely capitalists. So Lombard Street is "an organisation of credit", and:

> The main point on which one system of credit differs from another is 'soundness'. Credit means that a certain confidence is given, and a certain trust reposed. Is that trust justified? and is that confidence wise? These are the cardinal questions. To put it more simply - credit is a set of promises to pay; will those promises be kept? Especially in banking, where the 'liabilities', or promises to pay, are so large, and the time at which to pay them, if exacted, is so short, an instant capacity to meet engagements is the cardinal excellence.

For Bagehot, limiting the scope of the book to the money market was entirely justified because of the central role it played, and still plays, in the overall economy, not just domestically, but, because of Britain's dominance in world trade at that time. The London money market, Lombard Street, *mattered*. It was "by far the greatest combination of economical power and economical delicacy that the world has ever seen."

The trajectory of the book is clear. Because Lombard Street is so important, and because its whole raison d'être is credit, the key issue is the effectiveness and the 'soundness' of that credit system, which Bagehot describes as its delicacy. The maintenance of that soundness, and what should be done when its stability is undermined, is at the heart of *Lombard Street* and of its enduring relevance. It is not just a question of how to prevent 'panics' – severe runs on banks and the freezing of liquidity - but how to manage them when they inevitably occur, as they must in the real, imperfect world.

The British system was, for Bagehot, paramount because "English capital runs as surely and instantly where it is most wanted, and where there is most to be made of it, as water runs to find its level. This efficient and instantly ready organisation gives us an enormous advantage in competition with less advanced countries - less advanced, that is, in this particular respect of credit."

However, therein lies also the danger:

But in exact proportion of the power of this system is its delicacy. I should hardly say too much if I said its danger. Only our familiarity blinds us to the marvellous nature of the system. There never was so much borrowed money collected in the world as is now collected in London. Of the many millions in Lombard Street, infinitely the greater proportion is held by bankers or others on short notice or on demand; that is to say, the owners could ask for it all any day they please: in a panic some of them do ask for some of it. If any large fraction of that money really was demanded, our banking system and our industrial system too would be in great danger.

This analysis is at the heart of *Lombard Street*, and is what has been its most influential legacy right up to the calamitous events of the great Crash of 2007-09. Bagehot's prescription of what to do – from his late 19th century perspective, largely what banks, especially central banks, rather than governments, should do – has become orthodoxy – Bagehot's Rule - for central bankers and others, even if it can be argued that they often misunderstand or consciously adapt the details of his recommendations.

Because he believed that a panic, by its nature both irrational and rational at the same time, was "a species of neuralgia," therefore "you must not starve it." There must be a clear and sufficient source of bank reserves to be advanced freely to those in desperate need of it. "In wild periods of alarm, one failure makes many, and the best way to prevent the derivative failures is to arrest the primary failure which causes them."

His core argument was that the Bank of England must be the repository of that reserve. This issue had long been the subject of controversy among bankers and economic theorists, in which Bagehot had taken a prominent part. Furthermore, the Bank, as the nation's 'central bank', must be pro-active and use its position, when necessary, to prevent or mitigate bank panics, under strict conditions. The two main conditions were that recipients should have good security for the emergency fundings, and that the loans should be made at high rates of interest.

Throughout the book, he is clear that he is describing the reality of the existing system, not approving of, or prescribing, it. In his conclusion, he, in effect, admits that, if designing a new system from scratch, he would 'not have started from here'. The system was as it was, and has to be lived with, and the practice of all who participate in it needs to accept this basic fact, because it would not change, short of some external revolution. "You might as well, or better, try to alter the English monarchy and substitute a republic as to alter the present constitution of the English money market, founded on the Bank of England, and substitute for it a system in which each bank shall keep its own reserve. There is no force to be found adequate to so vast a reconstruction, and so vast a destruction, and therefore it is useless proposing them."

The extent to which Bagehot's thesis was, and remains, valid, and how and why central bankers, governments and others have had such recourse to it during panics and crises in the succeeding 150 years, is beyond the scope of this book. For present purposes, what is noteworthy is how key players in these existential dramas have followed – or claimed to have followed – Bagehot. The views and proposals of a country banker and financial journalist of the 1870s, someone who was not a trained economic scientist, have remained relevant, when so many similar tomes, written by eminent theoretical or professional economists and others – even those who have proved to be more technically accurate or coherent – have vanished into relative obscurity.

Professor Niall Ferguson, in his second BBC Reith Lecture in 2012 put it succinctly.

> In Lombard Street, published in 1873, the editor of the Economist Walter Bagehot described with great skill the way in which the City of London had evolved in his time. Bagehot understood that, for all its Darwinian vigour, the British financial system was complex and fragile ... No one has ever given a better description of how a bank run happens than Bagehot. Those unfamiliar with Lombard Street had to find out for themselves in 2007, at the time of the runs on Northern Rock and Countrywide - and again this year, when it was the turn of the Spanish Bankia to lose the confidence of its depositors.

A few examples from the recent crises should suffice. Mervyn King, Governor of the Bank of England during the early 2000s crisis, explained in 2010 the contemporary relevance of Bagehot:

> Walter Bagehot was a brilliant observer and writer on contemporary economic and financial matters. In his remarkable book Lombard Street, Bagehot brought together his own observations with the analysis of earlier thinkers such as Henry Thornton to provide a critique of central banking as practised by the Bank of England and a manifesto for how central banks could handle financial crises in future by acting as a lender of last resort. The present financial crisis dwarfs any of those witnessed by Bagehot. What lessons can we draw from recent and current experience to update Bagehot's vision of finance and central banking?

His counterpart at the US central bank, the Federal Reserve, Ben Bernanke, writing in 2019 about these events, described *Lombard Street* as "the bible of central banking ... and it's still a key part of the crisis response playbook. ... The Bagehot prescription was the necessary response to a liquidity crunch." However, he did, like King, recognise the limitations of the 150-year-old Bagehot analysis: "Bagehot's toolkit of central bank lending had limited value in preventing a run on a weak institution. ... Walter Bagehot had made the powerful case for why central banks should lend to viable firms against good collateral. This crisis illustrated the limits of Bagehot's doctrine."

Not everyone has been so enamoured of *Lombard Street*. A severe critic was the noted economist John Maynard Keynes, in a wide-ranging 1915 *Economic Journal* review of Emilie Barrington's 10-part collected works and life of Bagehot. After musing on the ambivalence of Bagehot as a writer on economic and financial subjects – "How is it that Bagehot was an economist and yet not an economist? How did he manage to write one of the classics of Political Economy, and yet appear to his relations no more than a brilliant amateur in a subject which he had chosen as a hobby while really a man of letters and very warm-hearted" – he then lays into the book itself, full of back-handed compliments that reveal his disdain:

> In form and intention it is a piece of pamphleteering, levelled at the magnates of the City and designed to knock into their heads, for the guidance of future policy, two or three fundamental truths. Incidentally, a great deal is described, and in terms which no reader, however little he understands it, can find dull. But never was a book written with less eye on examination candidates. The purpose was practical, and much of it has been attained. ... Part of it deals with obsolete facts and part with obsolete controversies, and a large part more is extremely difficult. I had forgotten how difficult the book is.

He does acknowledge the value of the book's core central bank focus and the handling of crises, which he regards more a psychological than an economic matter, but he dismisses other parts of the book as "not very good" or "rather confused and rather superficial." This failing he ascribed to Bagehot trying to deal with matters "outside the field of his own acute observation" or, in other ways, beyond him. Beyond *Lombard Street,* he dismissed some of his other economic essays in similar vein. The series on the depreciation of silver was "clearly second-rate, neither good theory nor good fact."

Informal government adviser

Initially through the patronage of James Wilson, and then through his own position as editor of *The Economist*, especially after 1860, Bagehot mixed in elite public circles in London. Not only was he gathering useful material for his work (at both the paper and the Bank), he was being sought out for advice by senior politicians and officials, especially on financial and economic matters.

Some of this activity was public, as when, like his uncle, Vincent Stuckey, before him, he gave evidence to parliamentary committees on financial issues. In July 1875 he gave evidence to the select committee on banks of issue, and in May 1876 to the select committee on the depreciation of silver. He even gave evidence to a French committee of inquiry in February 1865 on the circulation of money.

Most of his advisory activity was more confidential. It was said that Gladstone regarded him as a kind of 'Spare Chancellor', and Woodrow Wilson made a similar allusion in an 1895 essay, when discussing the influence of *The Economist* under Bagehot: "Its sagacious prescience constituted Bagehot himself a sort of supplementary chancellor of the exchequer, the chancellors of both parties resorting to him with equal confidence and solicitude."

Gladstone, as Chancellor of the Exchequer, discussing finance with Walter Bagehot

118

He enjoyed such a relationship with William Gladstone, who was both Chancellor of the Exchequer and Prime Minister at various times during Bagehot's tenure at *The Economist*. Their association had begun in April 1859 at a Wilson dinner party to celebrate the success of Walter's article and pamphlet on parliamentary reform. Writing to Eliza Bagehot on 12 June 1877 following Walter's death, Gladstone expressed his appreciation of the association:

> During the time when I was Chancellor of the Exchequer I had the advantage of frequent and free communication with him on all matters of finance and currency. Nor have I in all my experience known any one from whom in this important province more was to be desired, or who was more free and genial in the communication of his large knowledge and matured reflection.

Two examples of this association from the mid-1860s give a flavour of it in operation, and of the potential conflicts of interests arising, which clearly did not seem so ethically difficult then as they would nowadays.

Through 1864-65, Bagehot and Gladstone were in close communication over the question of the right of some country banks (such as Stuckey's) to issue their own banknotes, and the risks that may have for financial stability. Legislation had been mooted to regulate and curtail that right, with possible compensation through new rights for them to operate in London. The two had met on 3 March 1864, and Bagehot had given his views to the Chancellor, including a radical notion about State guarantees for such banknotes. Discussions continued for months until a Bill was eventually introduced in Parliament on 13 February 1865.

The country banks themselves had formed a committee to follow the Bill's progress and the Stuckey's Bank directors had Bagehot attend and report on its dealings, as Bank minutes of the period relate. With Bagehot wearing his editorial hat this time, *The Economist* published a series of articles on the Bill that spring, without revealing its editor's close personal interest in the matter. He did however disclose his interest to Gladstone during their frequent meetings and correspondence during that period, while assuring him, rather disingenuously, that he *really* believed what he was saying and, anyway, any true expert in a matter was almost bound to have some sort of interest in it. In the end, the Bill was withdrawn in June as no consensus could be reached.

During the Overend Gurney bank crisis, when that important bank completely collapsed on 10 May 1866, Bagehot wrote a hasty note to Gladstone the following day – 'Black Friday' - giving him his view of the state of the money market: "A complete collapse of credit in Lombard St. and a greater amount of anxiety that I have ever seen. ... There is much foreign money in London invested in bills--many due in May; I fear this money will be withdrawn from a general apprehension that English credit is not to be relied on." Gladstone had marked these missives "Mr Bagehot on the City crisis.'

For Bagehot, there was a more pressing matter, as Friday was the day *The Economist* went to press. He had to write instantly about the crisis. He produced two articles, one on the bank's collapse - where he coolly glossed over his earlier positive comments on the state of that Bank, implying he then knew something was amiss, but had no concrete proof – and the other on how better to mitigate bank panics.

Communication between Chancellor and editor continued in the aftermath of the crisis, and when Gladstone mooted to him the need for legislation on the country banks, whom he thought contributed to the crisis, Bagehot, being himself a senior country banker, swiftly sent him a long rebuttal on 21 May. Once again, he could, at one at the same time, be both the sage advisor and a business lobbyist.

Treasury Bills

One outstanding instance of Bagehot's advice being sought by Government and leading to substantive legislative and administrative change is the creation of the Treasury Bill in 1877. The detailed operation of such specific financial instruments as methods of short-term Government borrowing is beyond the scope of this book. What is relevant here is the key role Bagehot played in reforming and improving what was then an inefficient system. Until then the conventional method was the instrument known as an Exchequer Bill, but it had become inflexible and unpopular through the 19th century. Attempts at reform had failed and in 1877, the then Conservative Chancellor of the Exchequer, Sir Stafford Northcote, asked a senior Treasury official, Reginald Welby, to approach Bagehot for advice.

Bagehot had already addressed this issue in a short article in *The Economist* the previous September, succinctly entitled, "Why not issue Exchequer Notes at short dates?", arguing that shorter repayment dates on such credit instruments would be cheaper for the public purse and more popular with investors. Bagehot duly offered advice to Welby along his proposed lines, stating that the Treasury had the finest security in the world, but was not taking proper advantage, and a new, more flexible instrument such as a bill of exchange would be more convenient and familiar to the money market.

The Chancellor speedily accepted this advice, despite apparent resistance from the Bank of England, and legislation was introduced to Parliament in early February and swiftly passed by mid-March. The first tender for these new Treasury Bills was announced the day after Royal Assent, and it took place on Friday 23 March, just a day before the death of its inventor.

Bagehot did not claim or admit his role in this reform, even when *The Economist* wrote about it in February. However, in his Budget speech on 12 April, a few short weeks after Bagehot's death, Northcote did so, in what must be a rare example of mentioning a private individual on so important a financial occasion:

> I cannot avoid making a passing allusion to the name of a gentleman who took a great interest in this as in many other economical measures, and who, by his able advice, contributed not a little to the successful adoption of the scheme in question; but who has very recently, to our regret, been removed from us, and by whose death I am sure England has sustained a great loss. I refer to the late Mr Walter Bagehot, who was well known to Members of this House, and whose reputation extended over the country.

In a letter to *The Economist* in 1909, and in letters to Emilie Barrington in October 1912, Welby detailed Bagehot's role in what had proved to be a very successful reform. It was in one of these 1912 letters that he wrote more generally of his appreciation of Bagehot: "The machinery of our financial administration is complicated, and Mr Bagehot is the only outsider who had thoroughly mastered it. Indeed he understood the machine almost as completely as we who had to work it. This knowledge added to the soundness of his economical judgment, gave a special value to his opinion and advice."

The great economics book project

During what turned out to be his final years, he determined to produce a free-standing work on political economy. It would be a substantial work, divided into three parts. One would be aimed at bringing the tradition scope and methods of economics up to date in a manner suitable for 19th century Britain, as an economic and financial powerhouse. Another would be a review of classical economic theory of the likes of Ricardo, Smith and Mill. He had reviewed Mill's *Principles of Political Economy* in an 1848 essay, at the outset of his writing career. Finally, there would be his tried and tested device of examining a substantial topic through biographical studies of its major players.

In February 1875, he had hinted at his great project in a letter to the editor of the *Fortnightly Review*, John Morley, "I am writing, or trying to write a book on Political Economy which takes all my leisure (which is not very great), and I cannot think of any other subject till this task is done."

John Morley

He worked on this project throughout 1875, especially on his several summer holiday trips with Eliza around southern England, where, as has already been noted, he would usually work in the mornings, and spend the afternoons relaxing. By November, he was able to ask Morley if he could write a series of six or more economic articles for the *Fortnightly Review*, "on English Political Economy or some such title bringing out its position - or what I think its position - both as to the historical method and as to the mathematical which are now competing with it, besides some other things which I wish to say on the subject." He wished to retain the right to republish them as part of a book which "I have long been trying to write, but which I fear will never be finished except in pieces."

Morley was happy to accept his offer, and the result was a pair of essays entitled 'The Postulates of English Political Economy' in the *Review*'s issues of February and May 1876. Unfortunately progress from then on stalled. Whether this was due to increasing ill health and work and social pressures, or to a gradual realisation that the large and ambitious project as he had envisaged was actually beyond him, or not what he really wanted to spend valuable time on, cannot be definitively answered.

Again he wrote to Morley in June 1876, with a revised proposal, offering "a piece on 'Adam Smith as a Person' from me? I have it written and could easily adapt it, I think, for the Fortnightly ... The general conception would be something like that of the first article in the Economist this week" – he had written a short piece commemorating the centenary of Smith's *The Wealth of Nations* – "but grounded on biographical detail." At the same time he reported what progress he had made on the wider project, that he had a third article on Political Economy coming but not ready, and asked that the proposed Smith piece would also be available for inclusion in his economics book.

In her diary entry for 15 June, Eliza wrote, "Walter at home all day preparing Adam Smith article for the Fortnightly Review", and it duly appeared in the July issue of the *Fortnightly Review*, the last published section of the proposed magnum opus.

He had produced some drafts and 'fragments' over this period, which were found in his papers after his death. They dealt with various different topics, including 'The preliminaries of Political Economy', 'Adam Smith and Our Modern Economy', two profiles of Malthus and Ricardo, and pieces on 'The Growth of Capital' and 'Cost of Production'. Hutton and his former assistant editor, Robert Giffen, stitched them together, and published it all under the title *Economic Studies* in 1880.

Given its genesis, it is not surprising that it does not contain Bagehot's best work, even if he had had the opportunity to complete and polish these drafts. In that sense it was unfortunate that these were to be his final contribution to finance and economics subjects.

PART THREE

HIS COMMEMORATION

CHAPTER SIXTEEN
Preserving Bagehot's legacy

Introduction

Walter Bagehot's reputation derives primarily from his written work, and this was shaped by his life experiences. Since his death in 1877 the main focus of preserving his written legacy has been on collecting and publishing or republishing almost everything he wrote, including his letters. Biographers have used this body of work to recount and analyse his life, his beliefs and his impact on economics and politics in particular.

Over the half-century and more after Bagehot's death, his memory was perpetuated and his legacy preserved primarily by three people close to him – his widow Eliza, his great friend and colleague Richard Holt Hutton, and his sister-in-law Emilie Barrington. In this they had the willing support and cooperation of *The Economist* and its staff, who recognised the central role that Bagehot had played in its success.

Of the three, the key player was Eliza, as her diaries demonstrate. From Bagehot's death in late March 1877, she seemed to have dedicated her remaining life – which was to be a lengthy forty-four years – largely to her 'dear Walter'. She was the keeper of the Bagehot flame, the driving force in securing permanent memorials to him, like the West Window in Langport's All Saints' Church, and in the collection and publication of his numerous writings over a relatively short but extremely prolific career.

Perhaps this determination sprang not only from devotion to a husband who was taken from her unexpectedly early, but also from the memory of a similar sudden and premature death of her father, James Wilson, in India in 1860. James dominated his family of daughters as would be expected in 19th century society, and his loss was replaced in part by Walter's assumption of that 'father figure' role. So Walter's death could well have seemed to Eliza – and to Emilie and the other Wilson sisters – as some sort of tragic repetition of 1860. Westwater, in her 1984 study of the Wilson sisters, identified one strong motivation in relation to the loss of their father as a fear that he, and his achievements, would be forgotten by posterity. Just as they sought to perpetuate his life and legacy so Eliza and Emilie were equally determined to do the same for Walter.

Eliza preserved his memory in a very personal way, such as by having his writings frequently read to her, or by visiting his grave and memorial window at Langport Church. She also channelled her grief into more practical ways by preserving Walter's legacy for future generations to appreciate. Westwater's assertion that "Eliza lived only to perpetuate Walter Bagehot's name" may be an exaggeration, but not too much of one.

Three early outliers

In an obvious sense, Bagehot's body of work already exists in the various journals, books and pamphlets in which it was written. However, since his death there has been a desire, especially by his family, friends and admirers, to make these works much more accessible, as, of course, very few people would have had access to back issues of *The*

Economist, or the other journals he wrote for. They also wanted his works to be collected thematically. This began almost immediately, with a series of themed 'Studies', driven primarily by Eliza and Hutton, the latter acting as editor. The other main strand was a number of projects to provide more comprehensive collections of his output, beginning at the end of the 19th century in America.

However, it is convenient to begin with three discrete posthumous publications that do not fit easily to either of these strands, one which is not Bagehot's own work at all, but a collection of obituaries and tributes, and the other two which were unpublished at the time of his death.

The first was a pamphlet which collected his series of 17 *Economist* articles through 1876 on the topic of silver, as well as his evidence to a Commons select committee on the subject. In his preface, sent to the printers in early March, Bagehot accepted that the complex subject could not be completely covered by a series of articles, and that such a format is often disagreeable to read: "If I could, I would have re-written the whole of them in a more systematic form. But I have no time or strength at my disposal for such a task, and I am obliged, therefore, to use this substitute." According to a note in the published pamphlet from the office of *The Economist* dated April 1877, it was thought that Bagehot had planned to add to that preface, but no evidence to that effect was found in his papers. The pamphlet itself was published the following month, with the rather ungainly title of *Some articles on the depreciation of silver and on topics connected with it*.

Eliza's inscription on the flyleaf: From Mrs W Bagehot;
frontispiece and title page from Walter Bagehot: in memoriam, published in 1878

Next came a collection of notices following Bagehot's death, privately published and circulated in the latter half of 1878, entitled *Walter Bagehot: In Memoriam*. Eliza's diaries are the best source for this collection, and she noted on 29 May 1877 that "Mr [David Alfred] Aird", printer/publisher of *The Economist*, called on her in London "to propose to print & make small volume of notices about Walter." On 30 July she went to *The Economist* offices to hand over notices to use for the volume. Aird was summoned from London to Langport on 25 October about this project, as the entry in her diary for that day noted that he "appeared at 6 for instructions about the volume of notices about

Walter he is printing for me & returned to town at 7.20." Further correspondence took place over the following months about the contents and design of the small collection, followed by the process of proof-reading until mid-October 1878. Nothing is known about the print-run or circulation list of the volume.

The other outlier was an incomplete political essay written in 1874, the year when Disraeli's Conservatives took over power from Gladstone's Liberals, which was discovered in Bagehot's papers after his death. It was published in December 1878 in the *Fortnightly Review* (a journal in which Bagehot had published some of his most important work), then edited by John Morley, later to be a major Liberal parliamentarian and minister. It was entitled 'The chances for a long Conservative regime in England', and despite its obvious shortcomings, the piece was reviewed in several other journals of the day.

The thematic *Studies*

James Bryce, the Liberal politician who had befriended Bagehot in 1874, had responded to Hutton's 1877 obituary of Bagehot by suggesting to him that some of Bagehot's earlier writings, especially those out of print, should be republished. After all, he wrote with just a little hyperbole, "his study sweepings were better than most men's laboured works."

By the autumn of 1877, following such suggestions, lists of his various published writings were being gathered. On 28 November, matters had progressed sufficiently for Eliza to visit Hutton to sketch out the proposed two volumes of Biographical and Literary essays. Discussion of which works to include carried on into the New Year.

The focus through 1878 seemed to be on what became the 2-volume collection entitled *Literary Studies* (which contained a substantial introductory memoir of Bagehot by Hutton, dated 1 November 1878, but almost entirely reproduced from his memoir in the *Fortnightly Review* of October 1877), and it was proceeding towards publication by Longman by the end of the year. On 3 December, Eliza noted receipt of her first copy of the work, and it was officially published a few days later, receiving a number of reviews before the year's end. Almost immediately, preparations were being made for a 2nd edition, primarily, it appears, to correct various errors and misprints, and this was published by the autumn of 1879.

Also in 1878 work was proceeding on a collection of Bagehot's economic essays, again to be edited by Hutton, with various proofs being sent back and forth between Eliza, Hutton and the printer. However on 24 October she received a letter informing her that the collection could not be published at that time, though, unfortunately, she did not mention any reason she may have been given for the delay. Perhaps *Literary Studies* was taking up all the available time of those involved. Activity seemed to resume early in the new year, and there are many general references to proofs again being sent back and forth during 1879, some of which doubtless related to this economics collection

All this effort finally bore fruit, as on 8 January 1880 Eliza noted that the publishers, Longman, had sent her a list of those to whom they proposed sending the collection, some presumably for review. Two days later, she returned her specimen copy of the published *Economic Studies* to Longman. The following couple of months seemed to be taken up, as with the earlier published collection, in identifying corrections for future editions, and also receiving messages of thanks and praise from those who had been sent copies, or had reviewed it in print, where it had been generally well-received.

After *Literary Studies* and *Economic Studies*, the third and last of this set of themed collections was *Biographical Studies*. Eliza and Hutton had discussed such a collection in late November 1877, but further progress was not really noted until July 1880, when she offered Longman what she then called 'Biographical & Miscellaneous Studies', which the publisher promptly accepted. Work proceeded over the following months, much as in the manner of the earlier collections, with Longman trailing its imminent publication in the press, until finally, and doubtless with much relief, she received a letter from Hutton enclosing the last proof. In mid-January 1881 she had news from him of the binding of the new work, and it was published the following month as a single volume, again edited by Hutton, and again receiving generally positive reviews.

Amid the now customary post-publication process of identifying corrections for future editions, there was one innovation. In March, Hutton suggested to Eliza that she present a copy to the Queen and arrangements were made to do so via an intermediary, Sir Theodore Martin. He was noted in literary circles, and a recent biographer of the late Prince Albert, commissioned by Victoria herself. A copy was duly sent in June, and receipt acknowledged the following month, conveying the Queen's thanks.

Parliamentary reform essays

The final example of an early posthumous collection was a short single volume entitled *Essays on Parliamentary reform*. It contained the well-known 1859 essay from the *National Review*, as well as that same journal's 1860 essay, 'The history of the unreformed Parliament, and its lessons,' and was rounded off with the introduction to the second edition in 1872 of *The English Constitution*.

Unlike the three previous collections, it was published by Kegan Paul, Trench & Co and was not edited by Hutton. This time the initiative appeared to come from Eliza, who offered these essays to Longman in early January 1883. When they said they were unable to accept, she immediately turned to Kegan Paul, Trench, who accepted the proposal in early February, on payment by her of £50. After consulting with Hutton (then ill at home in Englefield Green, Surrey with influenza), she accepted their payment and royalty conditions on 14 February. Hutton collaborated with her on the proofs over the following months until October, and she returned the final proof to the publisher on the 12th. It was published the following month.

The Travelers Insurance Company collection (1889)

Perhaps surprisingly for a British writer, especially one whose published works had expressed mixed feelings about the United States of America, the first collection of Bagehot's writings was produced by an American insurance company, Travelers Insurance of Hartford, Connecticut. It was published in 1889. Fortunately, contemporary articles in the company's in-house magazine, *Travelers Record*, provide details of the origin and development of this project.

Travelers had been an innovative leader in the art of advertising its products and services, especially through free gifts, and its founder, James Goodwin Batterson, was a man of wide intellectual curiosity, especially in areas like economics. These two traits came together to create the ambitious plan to take the notion of promotional merchandising to a whole new level, by producing a collection of Bagehot's works as a unique way "to link the Company's name imperishably to a great classic, furnishing a historic memorial of our existence as long as the language shall endure."

The company set out a list of demanding conditions for the selection of the appropriate writer to be so memorialised, which unsurprisingly, combined high-minded altruism with hard-nosed commercial considerations. Or, as they put it, "Fortune and the strange caprice of the literary market have left for us an opportunity so ideal that t seems incredible even now that it is ours; at once so noble and so exactly within our reach, so fresh a boon to the public and so purely our own monopoly that Fate seems to have left it specially for us."

Forrest Morgan, editor of the Travelers Insurance Company collection

Bagehot met their criteria in terms of his literary greatness and, importantly for the project, in not being readily accessible to the general public in inexpensive enough form. Over two years were spent editing Bagehot's texts to make them suitable for such publication, and the travails of the editor, Forrest Morgan, set out in painstaking detail in his memorable preface, complaining about the state of Bagehot's original texts, have already been described in an earlier chapter.

The five-volume set was published in 1889 at the relatively cheap price of $5, and available only as a set. It would not be 'defaced with advertising', and 'the work is cheap in nothing but price.' Initially 1000 copies were printed of the self-described *The Travelers Ins. Co.'s Bagehot* – 'The finest library will not be shamed in placing this noble set beside the standard classics from any publishing house' - and a second edition, with minor revisions, was published in 1891.

It is not known to what extent, if any, Morgan liaised with Bagehot's family, friends and colleagues in the UK about his work. Unfortunately, several volumes of Eliza's diaries for the relevant years have not survived. However, those for 1889 and 1890, after the publication of the first edition, demonstrate some exchanges of correspondence between Morgan, Eliza, Hutton and Bagehot's publishers. Although the subjects of these letters are not detailed, there was some discussion about whether the British publishers would 'authorise' the US collection.

The Emilie Barrington collection (1914-15)

For such an important collection – 9 volumes of Bagehot's works, plus a biography of him – it is both surprising and disappointing that that there appears to be little on the record about its origins and preparation, especially the degree of involvement by his widow, Eliza, in what was published under her sister's sole editorship. The obvious sources are thin, especially Eliza's surviving diaries, where several key years are missing. Emilie Barrington's own introductions to the 1914 *Life* and to the complete 10 volume set the following year give few details. Westwater's work on the Wilson sisters virtually glosses over this surely significant event. There are some indirect clues in newspapers and other sources, but they pose more questions than they answer.

Emilie Barrington, Walter's sister-in-law, author of his 1914-15 Life & Works

The timing of the publication of these two works – 1914 and 1915 – does not seem especially significant in itself, not being any particular Bagehot anniversary. Nor is there any obvious explanation for the publication of her *Life* separately from, and before, the publication of the 9 volumes of *Works*. Was this her idea or that of her publishers,

Longman, the latter perhaps wishing to see the reaction to the *Life* before making the major commitment of a multi-volume set?

It is known from Eliza's diaries that there was a flurry of activity concerning a search for Walter's correspondence through 1905, which Westwater linked to the preparations for a *Life* of Walter which Barrington 'intended to write', though the diary refers simply to Eliza being interested in having the letters published. The sisters did spend time over the years working on Walter's letters and on his family tree, for example, and chunks of a *Life* – whether drafts of a work-in-progress or a near final text by Emilie - were frequently read to Eliza in 1912. Longman had placed a notice in the press in July of that year announcing the proposed Barrington biography of Bagehot, and asking for any relevant letters which may be of use to be sent to her at Herd's Hill. This again may have had an element of 'kite-flying'.

Perhaps the publication of the Travelers Insurance Co's collection in America rankled with the Bagehot family and spurred them to produce something more home-grown and 'official'. Barrington's preface to the *Works* acknowledges, in rather positive and appreciative terms, the Travelers collection, and states that her motivation for a new collection was to be even more comprehensive by including a selection of Bagehot's articles from *The Economist* (a paper founded and run in its early days, of course, by her father, James Wilson). She expanded on that in the preface to volume 9, where this new material appeared, claiming that these essays and articles "have, since his death, been entombed in old numbers of the Economist which but comparatively few possess, it is obviously right to rescue from oblivion a certain number by including them in this complete edition of Bagehot's works."

In the preface to her 1933 publication of Eliza and Walter's love letters, she wrote that "when my sister, Mrs Walter Bagehot, begged me to write the life of her husband, she entrusted to me all his correspondence ... at the same time appointing me her literary executrix." Eliza died in 1921, and her will was written in December 1918, several years after the *Life* and *Works* were published. So perhaps Emilie was referring to an earlier will or that she was informed in advance by Eliza of her proposed appointment. In either case, it is not known when this entreaty to write Bagehot's life was made.

In early 1911, Emile Barrington's *Essays on the purpose of art* was published, and reviewed by C Lewis Hind, who probably moved in the same artistic circles as her. In this review, Hind suggested that she might think of publishing a volume of Bagehot's works. Is it too fanciful to speculate that this might have been a scheme of Emilie's or even her publisher, Longman, to test the water? When Longman placed their request for assistance on material for the proposed *Life* in the press in July 1912, the reaction was not uniformly positive. One paper immediately responded by claiming that a 'family memoir' - and, implicitly, one written by a woman? - would be insufficient for such a figure as Bagehot, and hoped that someone like Lord Morley would take on the task "to do critical justice to Bagehot."

The love letters of Walter Bagehot & Eliza Wilson (1933)

In 1933 Emilie Barrington edited and published the 1857-8 love letters of Eliza and Walter. In the preface she explained that, as Eliza's literary executor, she came into possession of two locked boxes of love letters. She said that Eliza unreservedly approved of some of these, written by Walter, being quoted in her published *Life of Walter Bagehot* in 1914, and thereby justified publishing the complete set, 55 years after Walter's death and 11 years since Eliza's:

> I now, at this distance of time, assume sole responsibility for giving to the world all of them, written seventy-five years ago, and also those of my sister, by reason of their being unfettered revelations of their own inner selves, and, consequently, I hope, of value.

The Norman St John-Stevas collection (1965-86)

Some time around 1943 (perhaps not coincidentally, *The Economist*'s centenary year), according to *The Economist*'s editor between 1956 and 1965, Donald Tyerman, the then editor, Geoffrey Crowther, conceived the idea of a new collection of Bagehot's complete works. Apparently *The Economist* tried to do a deal with Travelers Insurance, who had published the first 'full' Bagehot collection in 1889, to produce a new edition jointly, but the American company declined.

In April 1959 Crowther approached Norman St John-Stevas to act as editor. Stevas seemed to be well qualified for the task. He had an academic background in constitutional law, and had just written a book on Bagehot, *Walter Bagehot: A Study of His Life and Thought*. At the time he was at Yale University, and so they met for lunch at the Yale Club in New York City. According to Stevas, others had been approached, but had declined the offer.

Agreement was reached on Stevas assuming the editorship of the project, along with a contract to write for *The Economist*, and he began in earnest on the mammoth project in the autumn of 1960. Over the next quarter of a century he worked on Bagehot, while pursuing a political career as a Conservative MP (since 1964), culminating in a Cabinet post during the first two years of the Thatcher government, 1979-81, as Leader of the House of Commons and Arts Minister.

He described his approach to the task in a note to the publication of the first two volumes in 1965: "My edition of the works of Bagehot does not set out to include every word he ever wrote. It does however aim to reproduce everything which could conceivably be of lasting interest." This required an extensive search of the existing sources, especially *The Economist* itself and other journals of the latter 19th century, to identify essays and articles authored by Bagehot – a not inconsiderable task when such works were usually published anonymously. This led to the attribution of much that had not been included in earlier collections.

The initial plan was a set of 8 volumes, divided by subject rather than chronology, inevitably an inexact approach given the scope of Bagehot's body of work, as earlier editors had discovered. There would be two volumes of literary essays; two of political writings; two of economic works, one of historical essays and a final volume of his letters and other writings.

As the research progressed this proved to be too modest a plan, as many new writings attributed to Bagehot were identified. Eight became 12, and by the time the final two volumes were published in 1986, the collection comprised a monumental fifteen volumes:- Vols 1-2: The literary essays (1965); Vols 3-4: The historical essays (1968);

Vols 5-8: The political essays (1974); Vols 9-11: The economic essays (1978); Vols 12-13: The letters (1986); Vols 14-15: Miscellany (1986).

Stevas wrote of the overall experience in a note in volume 14, 'On editing Bagehot':

> So for a quarter of a century Walter Bagehot has been my intimate if intermittent companion. While a member of the Cabinet the work crept along but I was able to apply much of Bagehot's teaching as Leader of the House. When I left office there was a great leap forward and now after twenty five years the edition is complete. I feel somewhat bereft - 'a labour of love' has been more than a tired cliche in this instance.

Norman St John-Stevas and his assistant correcting proofs at Herd's Hill in 1967

Research inevitably involved visits to the Langport area, of which some photographs survive. In fact, Stevas had already visited Langport in 1957 as part of his work for his earlier 1959 monograph on Bagehot, as he described in the *Collected Works*. This covered his birthplace at Bank House, Herd's Hill itself, and his grave in All Saints' Churchyard. At Bank House he saw the 1916 memorial stone plaque above the door, and was also shown the old strong room of the bank, which was connected by an iron bar to a room in the flat above which once belonged to Walter's father and was where Walter was born. Herd's Hill still had its impressive tiled fireplace by William De Morgan (now gone, unfortunately), and Stevas also viewed the steep steps through the garden which provided a short cut to the former railway station below. He was not impressed by the Langport Church window in Bagehot's memory, describing it is as being "of not very distinguished Victorian stained glass." At the grave, that same day (13 April), he picked a leaf, just as Woodrow Wilson had done six decades previously in 1896.

Each set of volumes was met with general acclaim as the realisation of *The Economist*'s, and Crowther's, original vision, and Stevas' achievement was lauded, especially in obituaries and tributes following his death in 2012. The 15 volume *Collected Works* is likely to remain the standard source on Bagehot for many decades, both in hard copy and in its full-text online version, posted by kind permission of *The Economist,* on the website of the Langport & District History Society.

To what degree the *Collected Works* contributes to the legacy, or to the wider celebrity of Walter Bagehot, rather than just being an invaluable resource for scholars and enthusiasts, is a matter for posterity. It was summed up by Ruth Dudley Edwards in her 1993 standard history of *The Economist*. When describing it as "*The Economist*'s stately tribute to its most revered name," she noted that "though well-edited, beautifully produced and a treasure-chest for those prepared to open it, the fifteen uniform navy-blue volumes did little to attract the unconverted. Like the editor of the Works, Norman St John-Stevas, the paper's luminaries sought to bring their great man to a wider public. Prime Ministers and ex-Prime Ministers were hauled in to pay tribute."

Prime Minister Margaret Thatcher speaking at the launch of the final volumes of Stevas's Collected Works in 1986

One especially interesting example of her last point was Margaret Thatcher speaking at the launch of the final two volumes at the offices of *The Economist* on 14 April 1986. This event coincided with the US bombing of Libya, using some planes based in the UK. This was a major political crisis for the PM, beside which a publishing launch must have seemed relatively unimportant. Nevertheless, she fulfilled the engagement, as she described in a US magazine interview a few days later:

> Even on Monday night, when I had to be at the completion of the Bagehot volumes, you know, our great editor of the "Economist" years ago, the great constitutional journalist, financier, we had ever had. I had to launch the remainder of those volumes with Norman

St. John Stevas. I had to make a speech. Nevertheless, I went to make that speech. I had taken endless trouble with it.

She recalled the event in her 1993 memoirs in an uncharacteristically ironic manner:

> That afternoon it was confirmed by telephone from Washington that American aircraft would soon take off from their British bases. I received the news shortly before attending a long-standing engagement at the Economist: this was a reception to celebrate the great Victorian constitutionalist Walter Bagehot or Norman St John-Stevas, his contemporary editor, depending on your point of view. As I entered the Economist building off St James's, Andrew Knight, the magazine's editor, remarked with some concern how pale I looked. Since my complexion is never ruddy, I must have appeared like Banquo's ghost. But I wondered how Andrew Knight would have looked if he knew about those American F1-11s heading secretly and circuitously towards Tripoli. Nevertheless I praised Bagehot, kissed Norman and returned to Number 10.

'Bagehotiana'

The diligent work of Stevas and his small team over the years yielded not just a treasure trove of Bagehot writings, but also a plethora of artefacts related to him and his family, acquired by, or donated to him and/or *The Economist*. This Stevas called 'Bagehotiana', and it included a collection of silver sold by Sotheby's in 1962. A selection, including items of Bagehot silver, his snuff-box, Eliza Bagehot's signet ring, as well as various certificates and letters, was the subject of an exhibition at *The Economist*'s London offices on 5-7 January 1966, accompanying the launch of the first two volumes.

An exhibition of 'Bagehotiana' arranged by Norman St-John Stevas in 1966

Some of this unique material was later donated by *The Economist* and by Stevas's estate to the Langport & District History Society, which puts on its own Bagehotiana exhibitions in Langport from time to time. In 2023 Bagehot's briefcase was restored for the History Society by the Leather Conservation Centre in Northampton.

CHAPTER SEVENTEEN

Commemorating Bagehot's life and work

Early memorials in Langport

There are no significant streets or buildings in Langport named after him, nor any statues or the like erected in his memory. Until recently there were only three memorials to be seen in his home town.

All Saints' Church West Window

It would appear that the idea for such a memorial came from the Stuckey side of Walter's family, very shortly after Walter's passing. Eliza's diary for Thursday 24 May 1877 records that, when back in London, she received a letter from 'Mr & Mrs Stuckey, Langport' which asked her if she would like to put up a memorial window in the west end of the Church.

This was the second Vincent Stuckey, the new Chairman of Stuckey's Bank, and his wife Mary, who lived at Hill House, opposite the Church (the former home of the first Vincent Stuckey). At that time the Church was undergoing extensive renovation, which was being led by Stuckey as churchwarden, and he himself had a new window installed in memory of his own mother. It would be very likely that the Stuckeys saw an ideal opportunity for a suitable, permanent memorial of this kind to Walter at that time.

Eliza immediately wrote to Walter's father in Langport seeking his view on the proposal, and when he wrote back expressing his approval, she replied to Mrs Stuckey the next day saying that she would put up a memorial window. This may have prompted her, when back in Langport afterwards on 13 June, to view the Church renovations, and also to visit Walter's grave for the first time.

Matters moved very quickly, with two of her sisters going to the workshops of Morris' and Gibbs' in London on 1 June to discuss stained glass windows for her. By the summer, Hugh Arthur Kennedy of London had been selected as the designer of the window, with Belhams responsible for its construction. On 17 June Eliza, Emilie and Kennedy were at Belhams' workshops to discuss the project, and two days later Eliza met Kennedy at Emilie's house to see his proposed designs. She wrote to Mr Stuckey on the 20th asking for measurements for the window. On 1 August Kennedy was at dinner with Eliza and her family discussing further his designs and drawings.

By 19 December 1877, Eliza, in Turin in the early stages of a 7-months-long European tour, had received a letter from her sister Emilie in London stating that she had seen the window completed. The *Langport Herald* of the 22nd, and other county papers, reported extensively on the erection of the new West Window under the Church's tower, giving details of the design. While she was still abroad, Eliza corresponded with Kennedy and with the Rev Lamplugh, curate of All Saints, in great detail about the protective wire being painted so as not to show through the window.

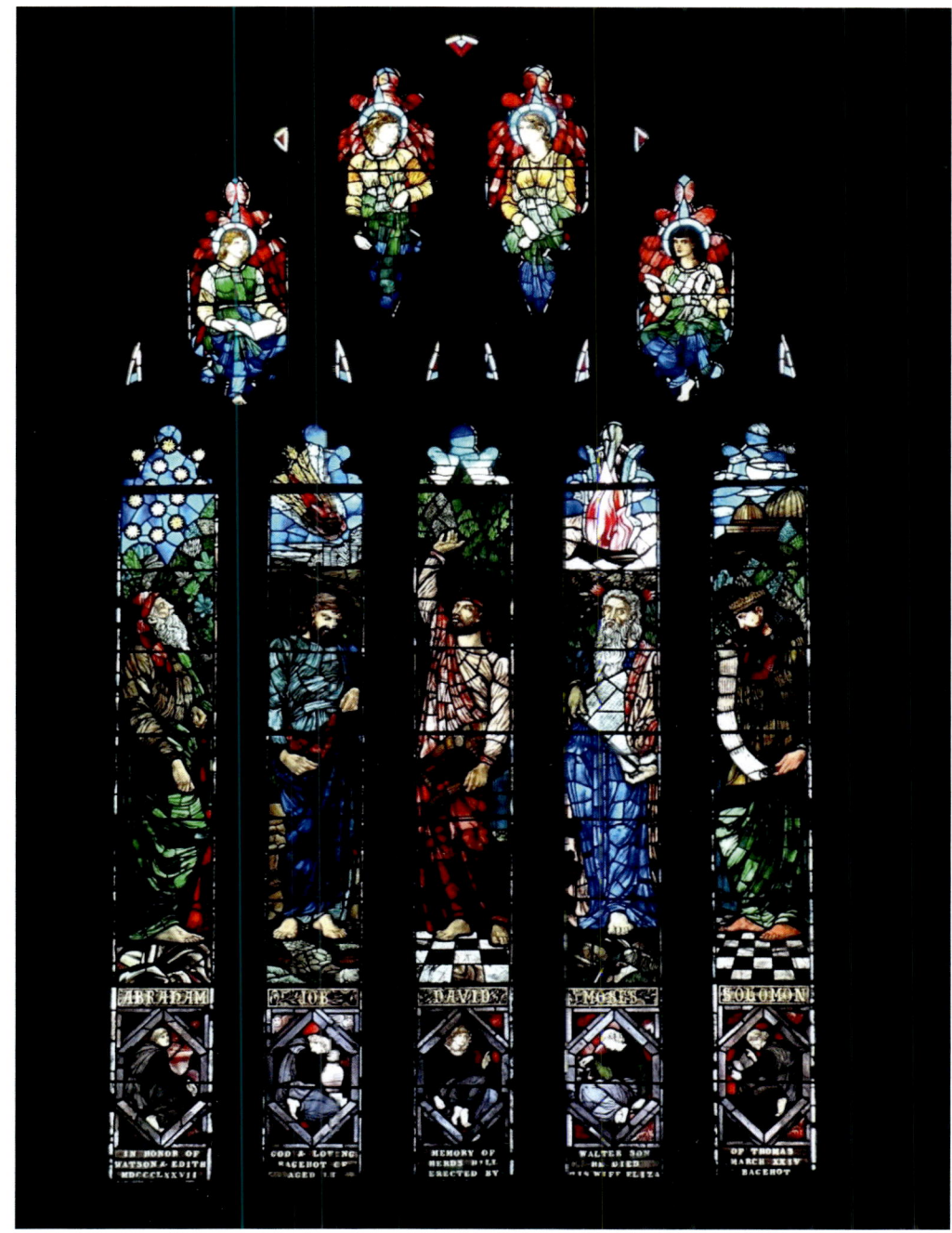

The West Window of All Saints' Church, Langport, installed by his widow, Eliza

After her return to Britain in late July 1878, Eliza and Emilie went to see "my window to Walter's memory" on 21 August during their first trip back to Langport, but she did not record her view of the memorial she had commissioned. However, clearly there were some concerns about it, though the diaries reveal no details, and after her mother and sister Matilda had seen it on 5 October, Eliza wrote to Kennedy "desiring him to make a design for altering window."

Kennedy worked fast and by 25 October Eliza drove to the Church "to compare Mr Kennedy's new sketches with my window," and on 2 February 1879, Kennedy called on

Eliza in London to show her his "fresh sketch" for the lower part of window. Things had moved on by the summer, when they finally settled on the alterations for the window.

By 3 November the altered window began to be set in place, and Eliza went to see it that afternoon. She watched the bases for the new window being unpacked on 26 November and they were put up on 1 December by Belhams. Eliza drove over from Herd's Hill on the 4th to see them in place, and twice more over the next two days. All that remained was the insertion of the new glass, which she saw in progress two days later. Finally, after several more trips to the church, she went with Mrs Michell (Walter's aunt) on 19 December to see the finished work, and, in a very rare expression of opinion in her diaries, declared herself to be "much satisfied with effect." With the memorial finally achieved, she promptly returned to London the next day, just as the *Langport Herald* was detailing the various changes made to the window.

The window was designed by Hugh Arthur Kennedy (1854-1905), and was made by Belham & Co, in their workshops in Buckingham Palace Road, London, using the 'antique glass' of Jesse Rust of Wandsworth (1825-95), which was admired for its unique qualities. This window is regarded as a fine and innovative example of Arts & Crafts stained glass. The original design is fully described in the *Langport Herald* of 22 December 1877, and the revisions in the 20 December 1879 issue. In its final form of 1879, the window displays five lights each representing a particular quality, in the form of a Biblical figure, as follows: faith/Abraham, resignation/Job, inspiration/David, Justice/Moses and wisdom/Solomon. An inscription at the foot of the Window states, "In honour of God, and loving memory of Walter, son of Thomas Watson and Edith Bagehot, of Herd's Hill; he died March 24th, 1877. Erected by his wife, Eliza Bagehot."

Bagehot gravesite, All Saints' Churchyard

The Bagehot family gravesite in the south-eastern corner of the churchyard is a Grade 2 listed structure, referred to in the official Historic England listing as the Bagehot Monument. The list entry gives this description: 'Tombstones and enclosure, 1877. Ham stone. Two matching headstones, with scroll heads and leaf side decoration, and in front square enclosure in Gothic style, open balustrading on plinth with coping, having quatrefoil and leaf decoration.'

The Bagehot family grave in the churchyard of All Saints', Langport

138

In fact the exact date or dates of the erection of the headstones and the surrounding stonework enclosure is unknown. References in Eliza Bagehot's diaries for 1889-90 suggest that there was substantial work done on the gravesite then, perhaps even the erection of the headstones themselves. An entry for 20 August 1877, just months after Bagehot's death, noted that she, her sister Emilie and the Stuckeys went to the church "to see the old monuments", which may possibly be a reference to original headstones at the Bagehot grave.

The people commemorated on the gravestones are:

On the right-hand headstone:
    Walter Bagehot (1826-1877)
    Eliza Bagehot, née Wilson, his wife (1832-1921)
    Watson Bagehot, his brother (1824-1827)

On the left-hand headstone:
    Thomas Watson Bagehot, his father (1795-1881)
    Edith Bagehot, née Stuckey, his mother (1786-1870)
    Vincent Estlin, his half-brother (1807-1869)
    George Stuckey Estlin, his half-brother (1809-1829)
    (Joseph) Prior Estlin, his half-brother (1811-1821)

Unfortunately two of the dates engraved on the headstone are incorrect. George Stuckey Estlin died on 10 June 1829, not 1 June 1829, and Edith Bagehot died 21 February 1870 rather than 21 January.

Over time this substantial gravesite had fallen into disrepair, requiring ad hoc work to maintain it, some due to the generosity of *The Economist* following requests by local people, mindful of the local importance of the Bagehots. Some of this remedial work actually caused new problems, because of the site's location in a corner of the hilltop graveyard, leading to pressure on the cemetery's outer walls, thereby potentially threatening neighbouring properties.

This led to a more concerted local effort in 2011-12 from the Langport & District History Society and Langport Town Council (the latter having responsibility for the maintenance of the churchyard) to provide a more permanent solution. This included repairing the stonework and re-lettering the headstones' inscriptions to something approaching their original appearance. This exercise was the catalyst for the formation of the Bagehot Memorial Fund, dedicated in the following years to preserving the legacy of Walter Bagehot, through exhibitions, writings and other activities in the Langport area. The Fund's mission is now a key part of the History Society's work.

A tradition has grown up of those visiting the grave in a form of 'pilgrimage' picking a leaf as a memento. The first notable example was in 1896, when the future US President, Woodrow Wilson, then a Princeton professor and great admirer of Bagehot, visited the grave during a cycling tour of Britain. From Langport, on 12 August, he wrote to his wife, Ellen Axson Wilson, in Princeton, describing his pilgrimage, closing with this request, "The leaf enclosed is from Bagehot's grave, darling; please press it and keep it for me." Sadly, the Wilson Presidential Library and Museum in Staunton, Virginia neither has the Langport leaf, nor any knowledge of its whereabouts.

Future President Woodrow Wilson visited the grave in 1896 and 1899

Eliza recorded that she picked an ivy leaf when she visited the site in March 1875, following the death in 1870 of Walter's mother, Edith. More poignantly, she picked another leaf when visiting it again in June 1877 for the first time after her husband's burial there two months previously. She also affixed a pressed dried flower picked from the grave on 1 November 1884 into her diary, and other similar floral insertions may also have been from Walter's grave.

The souvenir Eliza picked from Walter's grave and stuck in her diary

When visiting Langport in 1957, while researching Bagehot for a book he was writing, Norman St John-Stevas (later to be editor of the mammoth 15-volume *Collected Works*), also picked a leaf.

Stone Plaque, Bank Chambers

The third early Langport memorial is the stone plaque erected in 1916 above the front door of Walter's birthplace, Bank House, now known as Bank Chambers, in Cheapside.

It is a simple memor al, and had weathered badly since it was installed on 25 March 1916. Yet at the time, its unveiling was a notable event, and not just locally or in Somerset. It is not known exactly why the plaque was installed in 1916. It was ten years before the centenary of his birth, and was not a particular anniversary year otherwise for Bagehot's life and work. Possibly it was prompted by a revival in interest in Bagehot following the publication in 1914 and 1915 of Emilie Barrington's 10-volume *Life and Works*.

Viscount Bryce

The guest of honour at the unveiling was Viscount Bryce, who enjoyed a long career as a practising and academic lawyer, historian and senior Liberal politician, serving in several Liberal cabinets. Bryce first encountered Bagehot in 1874, when the Bagehots temporarily moved house in London to 52 Rutland Gate, and they met up one Sunday afternoon at the Priory, the home of 'Mr. and Mrs. George Lewes' ('Mrs Lewes' being the author, George Eliot). On leaving the house together, Bagehot invited him to come to Rutland Gate, which he did.

Emilie Barrington wrote to Bryce in 1913, following his return from Washington, where he had served as Ambassador, asking for his recollections of Bagehot for her proposed *Life*. He responded with a fulsome tribute, which Barrington reproduced.

On the great day itself, Russell Barrington, Emilie's husband, drove to Taunton to collect the honoured guests from the train, and brought them to Herd's Hill for lunch. The following day, Sunday 26 March, Emilie drove the Bryces and Francis W Hirst, who had been editor of *The Economist* since 1907, around the local sites like Burton Pynsent, and the Abbey and the Priest's House in Muchelney. After breakfast on Monday morning, the Bryces and Hirst left for London, but, as was common at that stage in her life, Eliza spent all day in bed.

The unveiling was reported in the national and local press, and the *Langport Herald* of Saturday 1 April 1916 described the ceremonies of the previous Saturday afternoon, 25 March, in great detail.

Memorial stone plaque on Bank Chambers, re-lettered in 2025

Before the unveiling itself, many local worthies, Bagehot family members and other guests gathered across the road at Langport Town Hall. Proceedings were opened by Col John Robert Phelips Goodden of Sherborne, the last chairman of the independent Stuckey's Bank, serving from 1902 to 1909. In his address, he said that, though he did not join the Bank until after Bagehot's death, he recalled meetings when the older directors would say 'Walter Bagehot's opinion was so and so', "and that was always quite sufficient to clinch the argument."

Bryce made the keynote speech in praise of Bagehot's memory. Bagehot was "one of the finest minds of his generation ... a mind of considerable delicacy and subtlety... There was no appearance of his exerting himself to be original and brilliant. Originality and brilliance came upon him as easily as the soil throws up flowers in the spring."

He praised Bagehot's influential writings, and most of all, the quality of his writing style, making his articles and books so readable, even those on the so-called 'dismal science' of economics. In conclusion, he said that "all the admirers of his writings and those who still remain who recollect his personal charm ... will rejoice to think this memorial of him is set up here in the county of Somerset among whose worthies he will always hold a leading place."

Hirst, in proposing a vote of thanks to him, also praised Bagehot, his predecessor as editor of *The Economist*. "It was a distinction to any town in the United Kingdom, however large, to have had such a citizen as Walter Bagehot."

Bryce responded to that Langport connection: "it was perfectly understood that Langport would always be associated with the name of that illustrious man. ... The town had a history of which it was proud [and] it was a proud thing for that little town to have produced such a man as Walter Bagehot."

The party then adjourned to the Bank House where Bryce unveiled the plaque, saying, "I now unveil this memorial tablet to a most illustrious citizen and commend it to the tender care of the inhabitants of Langport."

The rectangular tablet is made of Ham stone, with red lettering surrounded by a border of bay leaves in relief. It was produced by Messrs H Pittard & Son of Langport. It states: 'Walter Bagehot was born in this House February 3rd 1826. He died at Herds Hill, March 24th, 1877.' It was said to have been designed by Emilie Barrington, and Eliza's diary entry for Tuesday 22 February 1916 notes that they and Emilie's husband, Russell, went to Pittards, where Norman Pittard showed them the plaque, "and Emilie chose the shade of red for the lettering."

Who chose the text of the plaque is not known. It is certainly rather brief, with no explanation of who Bagehot was and why he deserved such a memorial. It would be nice to think that this was because at that time it was thought unnecessary to explain to the Langport of 1916 who he was. In late 2025, as part of the local History Society's activities to celebrate the bicentenary of Bagehot's birth in February 2026, it commissioned, with the kind permission and support of the building's present owners, repairs to the plaque, including the re-lettering of its inscription. Now restored to something like its original appearance, it remains an important memorial to Bagehot in his home town of Langport.

More recent Langport Memorials

Walter Bagehot Town Garden

Behind Langport Town Hall lies the Town Garden, reconstructed and given to Langport Town Trust by Tesco when they developed their supermarket in North Street at the turn of this century. In 2012, at the urging of local supporters of the fledgling Bagehot Memorial Fund, the Town Trust agreed to rename it the Walter Bagehot Town Garden.

Interpretation Boards

An early project for the Bagehot Memorial Fund was the design and installation of a series of Interpretation Boards around the centre of Langport, to provide key information for the local community and for visitors on the life, work and legacy of town's most illustrious citizen, in an accessible and engaging way. The details on the Boards were based on extensive research, and their design and their overall 'look' were in the hands of a noted designer, Belinda Magee, who had already completed similar commissions locally.

The first Bagehot Memorial Board, in the Walter Bagehot Town Garden, Langport

The first Board, '*Walter Bagehot - a Langport man – an international figure*', provides a general overview of the life and legacy of Walter Bagehot. Unveiled in the newly-renamed Walter Bagehot Town Garden on 25 March 2013, before a group of Fund supporters, including guests from *The Economist*, it has proven over the years to be a successful visual introduction to 'all things Bagehot.'

The second Board was unveiled on 3 February 2024, the anniversary of Bagehot's birthday, in the churchyard of All Saints' Church, Langport, where Walter, his wife and parents are buried. Unveiled by Cllr Sean Dromgoole, Chair of Langport Town Council, the board is entitled '*The Bagehots and the Stuckeys: two notable Langport families*'. It focuses on those two prominent Langport families, linked by marriage and by commerce, as well as the various connections between the families and Langport's Church.

The second Bagehot Memorial Board, in the churchyard of All Saints', Langport

The third and final Board was unveiled on the east wall of the former Great Bow Wharf warehouse at Great Bow Yard, by Langport bridge, on 18 October 2025. Entitled '*Great Bow Wharf: Langport's commercial hub*', it uses the building as a living symbol of Langport's former prosperity and importance as a centre of the commercial river trade on the Parrett and beyond – and the prestigious Stuckey's Banking Company that grew out of it, in which the two families of Bagehot and Stuckey were dominant players.

The third Bagehot Memorial Board, Great Bow Wharf warehouse, Bow Street, Langport

A London memorial

The blue plaque on 12 Upper Belgrave Street, London

In the mid-1960s, Norman St John-Stevas, Bagehot's biographer and chronicler, suggested to the Greater London Council that it should erect a blue plaque on Bagehot's London home, 12 Upper Belgrave Street, SW1, just off Belgrave Square. The GLC agreed, and on 26 July 1967, a blue plaque in Bagehot's honour was unveiled by no less than the Prime Minister of the day, Harold Wilson. It is thought that this was the first time a serving Premier had performed a blue plaque unveiling.

Prime Minister Harold Wilson unveiling the plaque

Wilson, himself an economist by background, was well qualified to speak about Bagehot's writing in the areas of both politics and finance: "Bagehot towered over the world of journalism and public affairs during his lifetime, and was the most acute observer of the political and economic society in which he lived... His important ability was his willingness to interpret established doctrines in new ways."

Other things named after Bagehot

One obvious way of both perpetuating the memory of someone and thereby recognising their 'claim to fame' is by naming things after them. Here are some examples.

Asteroid 2901

2901 Bagehot is a main-belt asteroid discovered on February 27, 1973 by the Czech astronomer, Lubos Kohoutek, at the Hamburg-Bergedorf Observatory in Germany.

Asteroids are named only when they have been observed enough times for an accurate orbit to be calculated. They are then given a catalogue number. Bagehot's number shows that it was the 2,901st asteroid to be formally identified. After that, the discoverer is allowed to propose a name.

In Bagehot's case, its discoverer had found so many asteroids that he had forgotten to propose names for them all. After ten years, such anonymous asteroids become fair game for other namers. The name of asteroid 2901 was proposed by a former science editor of *The Economist*, which Bagehot edited for 16 years. So Bagehot it became.

Knight-Bagehot Fellowships, Columbia Graduate School of Journalism

Columbia University's Graduate School of Journalism founded the Knight-Bagehot Fellowships in 1975 to improve the quality of the news media's business and economic journalism. The brainchild of its then Dean, Elie Abel, it was aimed at experienced journalists and reporters. It was originally named the Walter Bagehot Fellowship in Economic and Business Journalism. Since its inception, it has been a prestigious programme, and its graduates are known as 'Bagehots'.

It was named after Bagehot because in the words of Dean Abel, "Bagehot stood for the kind of excellence that ought to become a benchmark for American reporting." However, there was some initial controversy about the selection of a non-American, especially one whose name was hard to pronounce.

In a letter dated 13 June 1975 to the then editor of *The Economist*, Andrew Knight, Abel explained the choice rather more bluntly: "You may well wonder why an American university should have chosen to honor an Englishman in this way. The answer, regrettably, is that after searching our memories most carefully we were unable to come up with a single American journalist who personified the excellence we seek in the area of political economy."

Bagehot Lecture on History and Journalism, Queen Mary College, London

What was then Queen Mary College, University of London, launched an annual Bagehot Lecture in 2003 in conjunction with a new political journalism degree. It was probably the initiative of Professor Peter Hennessy (Lord Hennessy of Nympsfield), a renowned political journalist and contemporary historian, and his students who formed what was the Mile End Group at Queen Mary, now the Mile End Institute. It appears have lapsed around the early 2010s when the related degree was no longer offered.

An old QM webpage, no longer available, explained why it was named after Bagehot:

> The Bagehot Lecture ... was named in honour of Walter Bagehot (1826-1877), the greatest political and economic journalist of the 19th century. He wrote with brio and panache and his book The English Constitution virtually became the constitution. Bagehot's extensive knowledge of both the political world of Westminster and the financial world of the city made him an influential figure, influence which he exercised particularly through 'effective articles in great journals.' Walter Bagehot also edited The Economist with great distinction from 1861-77.

Bagehot Lectures at The Economist Buttonwood Gatherings

The Buttonwood Gathering was *The Economist's* flagship finance and economics event, held annually from 2009 in New York. The keynote address was entitled the Bagehot Lecture, named after the paper's most illustrious editor, and its lecturers have been heavyweight financial and banking figures such as present or former heads of major central banks like the Bank of England and the US Federal Reserve, senior finance ministers and leading economists. The 2010 lecture by Mervyn King, then Governor of the Bank of England, entitled "Banking: From Bagehot to Basel, and back again" was an especially influential talk, in the aftermath of the global financial crisis.

Walter Bagehot Prize, Political Studies Association

The UK's Political Studies Association (PSA) sponsors a wide range of awards and prizes, among which includes the Walter Bagehot Prize for the best dissertation in the field of government and public administration. Its website lists winners from 1990.

Walter Bagehot Research Council

There are various US-based organisations mentioned online which appear to be named after Walter Bagehot. It has not been possible to verify if they are one and the same organisation or several different ones. The named bodies include the Walter Bagehot Research Council, the Walter Bagehot Research Council on National Sovereignty and the Walter Bagehot Research Council on National Politics and Sovereignty (WBRCNPS) - which seems to have participated at annual meetings of the American Political Science Association – the Walter Bagehot Council and the Walter Bagehot Society According to various online sources, they were founded between the mid-1960s and 1972. The WBRCNPS was named after Bagehot, described as "the great British political economist and man of letters, Walter Bagehot, who founded and edited for many years

The Economist, one of the most important journals of the time, and who also wrote many literary essays."

'Walter Bagehot' pseudonyms

Writers on Bagehotian subjects, from politics to economics, have sometimes adopted his name as their professional pseudonym. Perhaps its most appropriate and prestigious use is as the pseudonym for the author of the regular, influential 'Bagehot' column on British politics in *The Economist*. The first 'Bagehot' was Michael Elliott, and more recent ones include Andrew Marr, Jeremy Cliffe and Adrian Wooldridge.

Another example was Jack Treynor (1930-2016), a well-known American writer on economics and finance, who published several economics articles in the *Financial Analysts Journal* in 1971-2 as 'Walter Bagehot'.

New Bagehot Project, Yale University

Yale University in the USA created the New Bagehot Project in 2017 to examine mechanisms of intervention in financial crises, prompted by the global financial crash of the early 2000s. It is run by the Yale Program on Financial Stability at the Yale School of Management. According to the Project's website it was named in honour of Walter Bagehot, whose Lombard Street is "the seminal text on crisis-fighting." It states that Bagehot's advice (or 'Rule' or 'Dictum') "is still considered near-gospel by many central bankers, but it is insufficient to guide the complex policy actions necessary to stabilize a 21st-century financial system."

Bagehot Rule or Dictum for central banks

At its simplest, *Bagehot's Rule* or *Bagehot's Dictum*, states that banks should lend freely, at a penalty rate, against good collateral. Although it has been picked over by many commentators over the decades, the Great Crash of 2007-9 and the main central banks' responses demonstrate that it remains their default position, albeit with added 'bells and whistles', often to deal with situations not known or foreseen in Bagehot's day of a far simpler, and much less globally interdependent, money market.

Bagehot Room at Great Bow Wharf, Langport

The Great Bow Wharf building in Langport, part of the site of the mercantile operations of the Bagehots and the Stuckeys, was rescued from possible demolition by a community-led initiative in the early 2000s to turn it into a multi-purpose space comprising a café, meeting rooms and office units. The two main meeting rooms are named, the Bagehot Room, and the Stuckey Room, and the offices are named after the major commodities which used to be traded on the River Parrett, such as Grain Store, Salt Store and Timber Store. While the Bagehot Room is named for the generations of the Bagehot family involved in these so-called 'Bridge Businesses', and not for Walter personally, he did play a part in these mercantile activities, and so is included here.

AFTERWORD

If nothing else, Walter Bagehot's was a singular life. He was acclaimed in his own too-short lifetime, and has remained an influential figure in many aspects of life since. He is not just an historical figure from a bygone century, but a person whose works remain relevant to this day.

This book has tried to illuminate the person behind the works, suggest why he should be commemorated, and how that has been done. Whether or not he should be in the top rank of historical luminaries, whether he was even 'the greatest Victorian', is entirely a matter for posterity.

What we have also attempted to show is that Walter Bagehot is not just a great British figure, but also a great Somerset person, and perhaps most of all, an important Langport person.

Lord Bryce said in March 1916, when unveiling the stone plaque in Bagehot's memory above the front door of Bank House in Langport:

> it was perfectly understood that Langport would always be associated with the name of that illustrious man. It was said in the Psalms that it should be said 'That he was born there' – and so it would be said of Walter Bagehot and Langport. The town had a history of which it was proud ... it was a proud thing for that little town to have produced such a man as Walter Bagehot.

Langport can be rightly proud of being the home town of such a such a unique and talented person as Walter Bagehot. For a small town with a rich heritage, having had Walter Bagehot as a citizen is arguably the jewel in its crown.

It is appropriate to end with a word from Walter himself, in his most frequently quoted – and sadly, but all too typically, most misquoted – line, written in 1853:

"The great pleasure in life is doing what people say you cannot do."

NOTES TO CHAPTERS

Foreword (p1)
'one 1960s writer described':- Jacques Barzun, 'Bagehot as historian'. CWWB vol3 p23

Chapter One: Why is he not better known? (pp9-12)
'one perceptive article in a 1908 journal':- F. C. Kolbe, 'Walter Bagehot: an appreciation'.
Irish Monthly, May 1908. vol. 36 pp282-7
'eminent historian of the Victorian era, G M Young':- CWWB vol15 pp207-13
'writer, historian and biographer of *The Economist*, Ruth Dudley Edwards':- Ruth Dudley
Edwards. *The Best of Bagehot*. London: Hamish Hamilton, 1993 pp4-5
'Roger Kimball':- Roger Kimball 'The greatest Victorian'. *New Criterion,* Oct 1998 p23
'Pope Paul VI':- 'Monsieur Bagehot and the Pope', *The Listener*, 7 Aug 1969
'solemn Victorian worthy':- Ruth Dudley Edwards, op cit, p1
'had I not survived him':-   EB *Life* p457

Chapter Two: Bagehot's background (pp13-17)
'Some sources claim :-CWWB vol 1 p30
'said to come from Prestbury':- EB *Life* p60-61
'arms of Bagot':- Illustrated in: *A collection of coats of arms borne by the nobility and
gentry of the County of Glocester*. 1792
'College of Arms':- letter to Michael Churchman dated 27 Sep 1971
'What can be substantiated':- Non-conformist registers of Castle Street Independent
Chapel, Abergavenny
'together they built up a thriving river trade':-*Victoria County History of Somerset* vol 3.
London, 1974. Langport, pp16-38
'Bagehot crest':- reproduced in the family tree of Bagehot and Stuckey, CWWB vol 15

Chapter Three: Young Walter (pp18-20)
'quipped in a 1977 article':- James Grant. 'Genius on deadline'. *The Alternative*, Feb
1977, p9
'Mary Watson Bagehot':- CWWB vol 15 pp312-5
'addressed to a great-uncle':- CWWB vol 12 p75
'Henry Sawtell':- Sawtell's 1882 letter to Eliza Bagehot, CWWB vol 15 pp5-8
'Lived much in his imagination':- EB *Life* p81

Chapter Four: Education (pp21-28)
'The education required':- CWWB vol 12 p166
'advertisement in a local paper':- *Sherborne Mercury,* 29 June 1835
'school magazine, *The Alfredian*':- *The Alfredian,* Summer Term 1907 pp2-3
'city guide':- John Chilcott. *Chilcott's descriptive history of Bristol*, 1840 pp207-8
'Fry later described':- EB *Life* p85
'Felt rather dismal':- CWWB vol 12 p155
'never been without fears':- CWWB vol 12 p255

Chapter Five: Turning point 1: Law, letters and Langport (pp29-36)
'turn your attention a little':- CWWB vol 12 p197
'Great Exhibition':- CWWB vol 12 p317

'letter to his friend Hutton':- Morgan Library & Museum, New York. Letter 26 June 1851, Accession number MA 13155 https://www.themorgan.org/literary-historical/393058

'he had been asked to research:- Grant p36

'According to Hutton':- R H Hutton. 'Memoir. *Fortnightly Review*, Oct 1877, in CWWB vol 15 p112

'considering carefully the question':- CWWB vol 12 pp334-6

'so swept up':- CWWB vol 1 p51, vol 12 pp323-9

'relationship with his father:- EB *Life*, pp210-11

Chapter Six: Bagehot in business (pp37-45)

'His 1873 'Wilson Memorandum'':- CWWB vol 14 pp419-26

'business is much more amusing than pleasure':- eg. Hutton, CWWB vol 15 p111

'He had 130 shares':- Grant p169

'took down young Mr Deedes':- Diaries, 12 July 1869

'l'affaire Badcock':- Diaries, 26 Nov and 19 Dec 1872. For Badcock's Bank's takeover by Stuckey's Bank in 1873, see Philip T Saunders. *Stuckey's Bank*, Taunton: Wessex Press, 1928, pp67-9

'lives of successful bankers':- *Lombard Street*, in CWWB vol 9 pp183-4

'Bridgwater focus':- Evidence to Bridgwater Bribery Commissioners, 13 Oct 1869. CWWB vol 14 pp339-40

'The Merchant's Function':- CWWB vol 14 p329

'Woodrow Wilson':- 'A wit and a seer'. *Atlantic Monthly,* Oct 1898, in CWWB vol 15 p130

'these more practical activities':- EB *Life* p208

'Robert Giffen':- Robert Giffen. 'Walter Bagehot'. *Encyclopaedia Britannica* 11th ed. 1910 vol3 p198

'little Cornish port of Boscastle':- CWWB vol 14 p117

'his only known investment':- Grant p283

Chapter Seven: Turning point 2: Eliza and *The Economist* (pp46-54)

'for the sake of holiday':- CWWB vol 13 p386

'very early published article':- 'The currency monopoly' CWWB vol 9 pp235-71

'tongue-in-cheek letter':- CWWB vol 13 pp390-1

'mother's mental illness':- Westwater p55

'George Ticknor':- EB *Life* p235

'Anne Beale':- 'Anne Beale, governess and writer: extracts from her diary. *Girls Own Paper*, 1901 vol 22 p598

'intense series of love-letters':- Emilie Barrington. *The love letters of Walter Bagehot & Eliza Wilson*. London: Faber & Faber, 1933

'His views on marriage':- Morgan Library & Museum, New York. Letter 26 June 1851, Accession number MA 13155 https://www.themorgan.org/literary-historical/393058

'used to say banteringly':- CWWB vol 15 p124

'Walter and Eliza's wedding':- *Langport Herald* 1 May 1858, EB *Life*, p256-9, CWWB v13 pp538-40

'If you live in the country':- CWWB vol 13 p447

'Bank duly obliged':- EB *Life* pp55-6

'very fine collection of public animals':- CWWB vol 13 p547

'He had even been vetoed':- RDE pp208-9; Letter to Mr Labouchere, 14 May 1856

'a sort of general superintendence':- RDE p212-3

'saw such people':- CWWB vol 13 p560

'The Government offered':- EB *Life,* pp34, 344, RDE p219

Chapter Eight: Running *The Economist* (pp55-61)

'Edward Robert Bulwer Lytton':- CWWB vol 13 pp634-5

'Charles Villiers':- CWWB vol 13 pp582-3

'Bagehot's office':- RDE pp403-5

'one man Royal Commission':- Alastair Buchan. *The spare Chancellor: the life of Walter Bagehot*. London: Chatto & Windus, 1959 p138

'Robert Giffen':- CWWB vol 11 pp204-6

'William Newmarch':- RDE pp275ff

'a recent analysis':- Andrew Odlyzko. 'Bagehot's giant bubble failure.' Revised version 8 Sep 2024. https://www-users.cse.umn.edu/~odlyzko/doc/mania16.pdf. Further revised as *European Journal of the History of Economic Thought*, vol. 31 no. 5, 2024, pp. 798-841 (part of a special issue devoted to the 150th anniversary of *Lombard Street*)

'men of theory':- CWWB vol 11 p228, *The Postulates of English Political Economy I*

'1873 Memorandum to the Wilson family':- CWWB vol 14 pp419-26

'Ruth Dudley Edwards':- RDE p316

Chapter Nine: Political ambitions (pp62-68)

'one much later critic':- CH Sisson. *The case of Walter Bagehot*. London: Faber & Faber, 1972

'more social standing':- 'The advantages and disadvantages of becoming a Member of Parliament.' CWWB vol 6 p55

'Emilie Barrington':- EB *Life* p386

'Metaphysical Society':- CWWB vol14 p47

'new London University seat':- EB *Life* pp291-2

'a worried Eliza':- CWWB vol 13 p561

'accepted his failure':- CWWB vol 13 p605, *Manchester Courier,* 4 July 1865, *Langport Herald,* 12 Aug 1865

'one scholar':- Jillian Rowe. *The parliamentary politics of Bridgwater. 1832-1869*. MA Dissertation, University of Essex, 1994 p127

'as he later described it':- CWWB vol 14 p343, Evidence to Bridgwater Bribery Commissioners 13 Oct 1869 Q41,994. For his election address and campaign speeches see pp356-70

'Appearing before the inquiry':- CWWB vol 14 pp339-56

'A curious indication':- CWWB vol 13 p633

'wrote a letter to Hutton':- CWWB vol 13 pp616-9

'In the autumn of 1868':- CWWB vol 13 pp631-2

Chapter Ten: In his spare time (pp69-81)

'broke the windows':- Westwater p83

'the tragedy of his life':- EB *Life* p66

'cup-and-ball':- EB *Life,* p253

'true gambler's spirit':- Westwater p182, EB *Life* p253

'pack of harriers':-EB *Life* p212

'an outcry locally':- *Sherborne Mercury,* 14 Feb 1860, *Langport Herald,* 12 May 1860

'first-rate judge':- EB *Life,* p79

'staying at Great Marlow':- EB *Life* p372

'confessed as much to Eliza':- CWWB vol 13 p400

'long-drawn out social occasions':- EB *Life* p267

'mutual friends':- EB *Life* p360

'he wrote to one of his sisters-in-law':- 1861, CWWB vol 13 p575 'our ball went off well':- EB *Life* p361

'Brooks's Club':- CWWB vol 13 p667

'elected to the prestigious Athenaeum':- CWWB vol 1 p74

'Royal Statistical Society':- *Journal of the Statistical Society of London*, Vol 27, Dec 1864, pp 582–3

'Political Economy Club':- CWWB vol 13 p601

'a parliamentary debate':- Parliament of Canada, House of Commons Debates, 3rd Parliament, 5th Session: Vol 2 p1892

'On the emotion of conviction':- CWWB vol 14 p41

'Orithyia':-CWWB vol 13 pp402-4

'According to Emilie Barrington':- EB *Life* p445

'I sat up late last night':- letter dated 14 Oct 1859, CWWB vol 13 p553

'Walter 'fathered' it':- EB *Life* p406

'proposed a motion':- *Wells Journal,* 7 Jan 1865; *Bath Chronicle,* 6 Apr 1865

'annual congress':-*Langport Herald,* 31 Aug 1861, https://sanhs.org/wp-content/uploads/2019/09/03FirstExcursion-1.pdf

'Walter made a few remarks':- *Langport Herald*, 31 Aug 1861

'gave a lecture':- EB *Life* p364, *Langport Herald,* 8 Feb 1862, *Sherborne Mercury,* 11 Feb 1862

'houses and banking together':- CWWB vol 13 p481

'Bella Vista is ravishing':- CWWB vol 13 p480

'composing the drawing-room':- EB *Life,* p442

'sample-threads':- EB *Life* p443

Chapter Eleven: Final days (pp82-88)
'out of the fuss of the front door':- EB *Life* pp452-3

'write a letter in pencil':- CWWB vol 13 p679

'Robert Giffen':- CWWB vol 13 p677-8

'something of a shock':- Westwater p87

'One bizarre episode':- For example, *Monmouthshire Merlin,* 8 June 1877

'Emilie wrote':- EB *Life* p454

'Walter wrote a will':- CWWB vol 15 pp323-4

'Even the Government itself joined in':- CWWB vol 15 p55

'the most notable':- CWWB vol 15 pp62-3

'probably best expressed':- CWWB vol 15 pp53-4

'Walter's only surviving parent':- EB *Life* p457

Chapter Twelve: Bagehot the person (pp89-96)
'overall description':- CWWB vol 15 p1

'very fine skin':- EB *Life* p231

'overhanging thatch':- EB *Life* p62 (Henry Sawtell, 1882 letter to Eliza Bagehot)

'tuft of hair':- CWWB vol 13 p488

'eyes':- EB *Life* p231

'rather thin':- EB *Life* p85

'currency people':-CWWB vol 3 p443

'Recollecting her first sight':- EB *Life* p230

'very tiny notebook':- Emilie Barrington. *The servant of all.* vol 2, London: Longman, Green, 1927 p137

'exasperating':- EB *Life* pp357-8

sniffing the air':- EB *Life* p231

'liked to talk':- CWWB vol 15 p173

'old Langport woman':- Alastair Buchan, op cit. p194
'periods of financial calm':- CWWB vol 13 p457
'his friends smiled':- Grant p283
'anti-spending instinct':- CWWB vol 15 pp120-1
'political sobriety':- CWWB vol 15 pp128
'lost his train':- Diaries 13 Dec 1859, 3 July 1861, for example
'jokingly blamed Eliza':- CWWB vol 13 p455
'vault over the sofa':- CWWB vol 13 p402
'Westwater observed':-Westwater, p76
'Emilie described':- EB *Life* p411
'come and nurse him':- EB *Life* p410
'The diaries recount':- Diaries, 21 Sep 1866, 25 Aug 1871, 24 Sep 1867
'dentist's waiting-room':- CWWB vol 1 p194
'Smith's library':- EB *Life* p414
'to gain more profit':- CWWB vol 15 pp70, 125
'conversation notable':- EB *Life* pp354-5
'think or laugh':- CWWB vol 15 p124
'what a nut felt':- CWWB vol 15 pp13, 14
'talk theology':- CWWB vol 13 p443

Chapter Thirteen: Bagehot the writer (pp99-106)
'in his 1852 Hartley Coleridge essay':- CWWB vol 1 p159
'Emily Eden':- CWWB vol 2 pp168-73
'greatest living writer of fiction':- 'Sterne and Thackery' CWWB vol 2 p289
'William Haley':- CWWB vol 1 pp84-106
'I am afraid I covet':- CWWB vol 13 p413
'Clarity was an essential aim':- CWWB vol 1 p157
'Martha Westwater':- Sister Martha Westwater. *Walter Bagehot: the conservatism of a Victorian liberal*. PhD Thesis, Dalhousie University, Canada, 1973 p31
'Robert Giffen':- CWWB vol 11, pp207-8
'in full flow':- CWWB vol 9 p273
'James Grant':- Grant p108
'The great change of late':- CWWB vol 13 p557
'writing carelessly':- EB *Life* pp148-9
'St John-Stevas':- CWWB vol 12 p72
'Richard Holt Hutton':- CWWB vol 15 pp111-2
'numerical lapses':- CWWB vol 15 p68
'Forrest Morgan':- *The Works of Walter Bagehot,* edited by Forrest Morgan. 5 vols. Hartford, CT: Travelers Insurance Company, 1889 vol 1, editor's preface
'Bagehot's shortcomings':- Grant p292
'As to holidays':- CWWB vol 13 p386
'It moves my bitter envy':- CWWB vol 13 p581
'carried his mind':- EB *Life* p432
'holiday writing habit':- EB *Life* p405
'tedious repetition':- CWWB vol 7 p134
'a production not of science':- Grant pp240, 245

Chapter Fourteen: Government, politics and the constitution (pp107-112)
'essay on Gladstone':- CWWB vol 3 p415
'Living really in the political world':- Emilie Barrington. *The servant of all.* op.cit. p137
'division of the components':- CWWB vol 5 p206

'efficient secret':- CWWB vol 5 pp210, 212
'use of the Queen':- CWWB vol 5 p226
'A family on the throne':- CWWB vol 5 p229
'retired widow':- CWWB vol 5 p226
'poke about':- CWWB vol 5 p243
'three limited but essential rights':- CWWB vol 5 p253
'deeper lack':- CWWB vol 15 p167
'put it rather neatly':- Ghita Iorescu. 'The Shrinking World of Bagehot'. *Government and Opposition*, 1975 vol 10 pp1-11
'What would Bagehot say?':- BBC Sounds, www.bbc.co.uk/programmes/b09jdc7q

Chapter Fifteen: Banking and finance (pp113-122)
'most original writing':- CWWB vol 15 p121
'outside their normal range':- CWWB vol 15 p84
'Robert Peston':- British banks bailed out. BBC blog, 3 Oct 2008: www.bbc.co.uk/blogs/thereporters/robertpeston/2008/10/british_banks_bailed_out.html?
'near-literature of high journalism':- Grant p293
'little book':- CWWB vol 9 p46
'concrete realities':- CWWB vol 9 p48
'high-water mark':- CWWB vol 11 p215
'grand tour':- Grant p272
'organisation of credit':- CWWB vol 9 pp58-9
'lies also the danger':- CWWB vol 9 p56
'a species of neuralgia':- CWWB vol 9 p73
'substitute a republic':- CWWB vol 9 p214
'Niall Ferguson':- Niall Fergusson. 'The Darwinian economy'. 2nd Reith Lecture 2012, 26 June 2012, transcript:
www.bbc.co.uk/programmes/articles/3XhZsLTM18KBQX6C97w8K6z/niall-ferguson-the-darwinian-economy
'Mervyn King':- Mervyn King. 'Banking: From Bagehot to Basel, and Back Again'. Second Bagehot Lecture, Buttonwood Gathering: New York City, 25 Oct 2010. transcript:
www.bankofengland.co.uk/-/media/boe/files/speech/2010/banking-from-bagehot-to-basel-and-back-again-speech-by-mervyn-king.pdf
'Ben Bernanke':- Ben Bernanke et al. *Firefighting: the financial crisis and its lessons*. New York: Penguin Books, 2019 pp34-48
'Keynes':- J M Keynes, review of E Barrington. *The works and life of Walter Bagehot*, *The Economic Journal*, Vol. 25, 1915 pp369-72
'Woodrow Wilson':- CWWB vol 15 p157
'Gladstone expressed his appreciation':- EB *Life* pp457-8
'Through 1864-65':- Grant pp120-4
'Overend Gurney':- CWWB vol 13 pp608-10
'Treasury Bills':- Grant pp289-90, CWWB vol 15 pp55-60
'his great project':- CWWB vol 13 pp665, 672-3, 676-7

Chapter Sixteen: Preserving Bagehot's legacy (pp125-135)
'the same for Walter':- Westwater pp 21, 71-2, 88-9, 226
'topic of silver':- Stevas has two listings of these articles in his CWWB, with different dates for some and a different total, 17 in vol 10 p137, but 16 in Vol 15 p423.
'incomplete political essay':- CWWB vol 7 pp225, 240
'study sweepings':- EB *Life* p33

'the first collection':- CWWB vol 15 pp442-3

'strange caprice':- *Travelers Record* vol 24, Dec 1888, p5

'defaced with advertising':- *Travelers Record* vol 24, Jan 1889, p5

'a notice in the press':- *Westminster Gazette* 3 July 1912, for example

'Barrington's preface':- Emilie Barrington. *The works of Walter Bagehot*. London: Longman, Green, 1915 vol 1, preface ppv-vi

'new material appeared':- Emilie Barrington. *The works of Walter Bagehot*. London: Longman, Green, 1915, vol 9, preface ppv-xii

'begged me to write':- Emilie Barrington. *The love-letters of Walter Bagehot and Eliza Wilson*. London: Faber & Faber, 1933 preface, p9

'In early 1911':- C Lewis Hind. 'A little tale &c.'. *London Daily Chronicle,* 8 Feb 1911

'immediately responded':- *Pall Mall Gazette*, 3 July 1912

'she explained that':- Emilie Barrington. *The love-letters of Walter Bagehot and Eliza Wilson*. London: Faber & Faber, 1933 preface, p9

'Some time around 1943':-Donald Tyerman. 'Coping stones'. *The Economist*, 28 Oct 1978, p125

'tried to do a deal':- James Grant. 'Genius on deadline.' *The Alternative* Feb 1977, p10

'Crowther approached Norman St John-Stevas':- CWWB vol 14 pp1-2

'described his approach':- CWWB vol 1 pp15-6

'overall experience':- CWWB vol 14 pp2-3. Norman St John-Stevas. 'Twenty-five years with a patron saint'. *Sunday Times* 13 Apr 1986

'visits to the Langport area':- CWWB vol 14 pp4-5

'he picked a leaf':- CWWB vol 15 p307

'stately tribute':- RDE p228

'Margaret Thatcher':- 'She reads him, too'. *The Economist* 19 Apr 1986, p30

'US magazine interview':- Transcript of interview with *Parade*, given on 17 Apr 1986, published on 13 July 1986: www.margaretthatcher.org/document/106228

'recalled the event':- Margaret Thatcher. *The Downing Street Years*. London: Harper Collins, 1993 pp446-7

'subject of an exhibition':- CWWB vol 15 pp383-5

Chapter Seventeen: Commemorating Bagehot's life and work (pp136-148)

'Arts & Crafts stained glass':- Peter Cormack. *Arts and Crafts Stained Glass*. New Haven and London: Yale University Press, 2015; Peter Burnett. 'Walter Bagehot Memorial Window, All Saints' Langport'. LDHS *Level Talk* 2016, pp9-11

'official Historic England listing':- www.historicengland.org.uk/

'two of the dates':- 'A grave mistake'. *Local History News*, No. 141, Autumn 2021 p15

'was the catalyst':- 'Bagehot Memorial Fund', www.langportheritage.org.uk/walter-bagehot/bagehot-memorial-fund

'he wrote to his wife':- *The Papers of Woodrow Wilson, Vol 9: 1894-1896*. Princeton, NJ: Princeton University Press, 1971 p565

'also picked a leaf':- CWWB vol 15 p307

'first encountered Bagehot':- EB *Life* p441

'wrote to Bryce':- EB *Life* pp33-6

'blue plaque':- CWWB vol 15 pp319-22

'Harold Wilson':- CWWB vol 15 pp216-9

'asteroid2901':- www.spacereference.org/asteroid/2901-bagehot-1973-dp

'founded the Knight-Bagehot fellowships':- Columbia University Press Release, 11 June 1975

'From Bagehot to Basel':- Mervyn King, loc cit.

'The WBRCNPS was named after Bagehot':- www.anneandhenrypaolucci.com/about-him
'Jack Treynor':- www.afajof.org/wp-content/uploads/files/in-memoriam/IN_MEMORIAM_TREYNOR.pdf
'New Bagehot Project':- www.newbagehot.yale.edu/about/project
'Bagehot Room':- www.greatbow.org.uk

Other recent sources consulted

Volume 15 of the Stevas Collection provides a long, comprehensive list of other publications, some of the more relevant of which we have consulted for this book. As this is available online at the LDHS website, we do not seek to reproduce a secondary sources list, other than the following examples published since Stevas's list:

Norman St John-Stevas. *The Omnipresence of Walter Bagehot*. Oxford: Clarendon Press, 1987.

Ruth Dudley Edwards. *The Best of Bagehot*. London: Hamish Hamilton, 1993.

Frank Prochaska. *The Memoirs of Walter Bagehot*. New Haven: Yale University Press, 2013.

Janet Seaton & Barry Winetrobe. *Hurds Hill: a brief history of the family home of Walter Bagehot*. Langport: CreateSpace, 2014.

Alexander Zevin. *Liberalism at large: the world according to The Economist*. London: Verso, 2019

Michael Churchman. *The Stuckeys of Somerset*. Bryn Mawr: Privately published Revised edition, 2021.

ACKNOWLEDGMENTS

We wish to record our deep gratitude to those who have assisted us in our 'Bagehot' activities. These include all those in the local community – especially Langport Town Council (including its former Clerk, David Mears) and Langport Town Trust; Andrew Lee of the *Langport Leveller/Somerset Confidential*; Clifford Lee and David Holmes, present owners of the Bagehot family home, Hurds Hill, and the Heim family, owners of Bagehot's birthplace - who were heavily involved in getting these efforts off the ground a decade and more back, and ever since. We would also like to thank those connected with other places relevant to the Bagehot story, including the Warehouse Trust at Great Bow Wharf, and Langport's All Saints' Church. Last, but by no means least, we are very grateful to the Trustees and members of the Langport & District History Society, without whom none of this would have been possible.

Further afield, *The Economist* has been central to preserving the memory of its most illustrious editor. Special thanks go to a former editor, John Micklethwait and the current editor, Zanny Minton Beddoes, the late Helen Mann, its archivist, and also to its recent biographer, Ruth Dudley Edwards, without whose active support and generous donations of time and Bagehot material our efforts would have been so much less productive. Norman St John-Stevas, Lord St John of Fawsley, supported our Bagehot work in his final years, and his estate generously donated much of his extensive collection of what he called 'Bagehotiana' to our stewardship.

Michael and Jean Churchman of Pennsylvania (Bagehot and Stuckey family historians), and James Grant of New York, Bagehot's most recent biographer, have been strong sources of support and encouragement over the years. We are also grateful for the assistance of the many repositories of relevant material around the UK and beyond, including the Somerset Heritage Centre in Taunton, the National Archives at Kew, the British Library, University College London, the archives of the NatWest Group, and, in the USA, the Library of Congress, National Archives and the Woodrow Wilson Presidential Library and Museum of Staunton, Virginia.

Belinda Magee has been a brilliant designer of our various Bagehot productions, including our series of three Interpretation Boards in Langport. Her advice and assistance have been invaluable, not least on this book, whose covers she designed. A local artist, and good friend, Mike Sammons, has produced a delightful set of original illustrations which have greatly enhanced the unique and engaging look of this book. We would also like to thank Fran Atkins, Sonja Alves and Gael Lewis for permission to reproduce the images of Joseph Prior Estlin, Forrest Morgan and Dr Charles Coffin, respectively.

Grateful thanks are also due to Dr Geoff Lindsey, of English Speech Services, for his expert advice on the pronunciation of 'Bagehot'. Special mention should be made of Andrew Lee, who bravely read through a first full draft of this book, and whose comments, corrections and suggestions were priceless.

Finally, we welcome any feedback, whether to point out any errors or omissions, or to offer new information, and we are, of course, responsible for any errors in this book.

INDEX

161